On Freedom

By the same author:

On Freedom

KRISHNAMURTI

LONDON
VICTOR GOLLANCZ LTD
1992

First published in Great Britain 1992
by Victor Gollancz Ltd
14 Henrietta Street, London WC2E 8QJ

For additional information, write to:
Krishnamurti Foundation Trust, Ltd.
Brockwood Park, Bramdean, Hants, England SO24 0LQ

or

Krishnamurti Foundation of America
P.O. Box 1560
Ojai, CA 93023, United States

Sources and acknowledgments can be found on page 149.

Series editor: Mary Cadogan

Associate editors: Ray McCoy and David Skitt

A catalogue record for this book is available
from the British Library

ISBN 0 575 05328 3

Printed and bound in Finland by
Werner Söderström OY

Economically, you can, perhaps, arrange the world so that man can be more comfortable, have more food, clothing, and shelter, and you may think that is freedom. Those are necessary and essential things, but that is not the totality of freedom. Freedom is a state and quality of mind.

Poona, 21 September 1958

Contents

On Freedom

Foreword

JIDDU KRISHNAMURTI was born in India in 1895 and, at the age of thirteen, taken up by the Theosophical Society, which considered him to be the vehicle for the "world teacher" whose advent it had been proclaiming. Krishnamurti was soon to emerge as a powerful, uncompromising, and unclassifiable teacher, whose talks and writings were not linked to any specific religion and were neither of the East nor the West but for the whole world. Firmly repudiating the messianic image, in 1929 he dramatically dissolved the large and monied organization that had been built around him and declared truth to be "a pathless land," which could not be approached by any formalized religion, philosophy, or sect.

For the rest of his life he insistently rejected the guru-status that others tried to foist upon him. He continued to attract large audiences throughout the world but claimed no authority, wanted no disciples, and spoke always as one individual to another. At the core of his teaching was the realization that fundamental changes in society can be brought about only by a transformation of individual consciousness. The need for self-knowledge and an understanding of the restrictive, separative influences of religious and nationalistic conditionings, was constantly stressed. Krishnamurti pointed always to the urgent need for openness, for that "vast space in the brain in which there is unimaginable energy." This seems to have been the wellspring of his own creativity and the key to his catalytic impact on such a wide variety of people.

He continued to speak all over the world until he died in 1986 at the age of ninety. His talks and dialogues, journals and letters have been collected into more than sixty books. From that vast body of teachings this series of theme books has been compiled. Each book in the series focuses on an issue that has particular relevance and urgency in our daily lives.

Bombay, 7 March 1948

How is one to transform, to bring about this radical change from becoming to being? A person who is becoming and therefore striving, struggling, battling with himself—how is such a person to know that state of being that is virtue, that is freedom? I hope I am making the question clear. That is, I have been struggling for years to become something: not to be envious, to become non-envious. And how am I to shed, to drop the struggle, and just be? Because, as long as I struggle to become what I call righteous, I am obviously setting up a process of self-enclosure; and there is no freedom in enclosure. So all that I can do is to be aware, passively aware, of my process of becoming. If I am shallow, I can be passively aware that I am shallow, without the struggle to become something. If I am angry, if I am jealous, if I am unmerciful, envious, I can just be aware of that and not contend with it. The moment we contend with a quality, we give emphasis to the struggle, and therefore strengthen the wall of resistance. This wall of resistance is considered righteousness, but for a righteous man, truth can never come into being. It is only to the free man that truth can come, and to be free, there cannot be the cultivation of memory, which is righteousness.

So one has to be aware of this struggle, of this constant battle. Just be aware without contention, without condemnation, and if you are truly watchful, passively yet alertly aware, you will find that envy, jealousy, greed, violence, and all these things drop away, and there comes order—quietly, speedily, there comes order that is not righteous, that is not enclosing. For virtue is freedom, it is not a process of enclosure. It is only in freedom that truth can come into being. Therefore, it is essential to be virtuous, not righteous, because virtue brings order. It is only the righteous man that is confused, that is in conflict; it is only the righteous man that develops his will as a means of resistance, and a man of will can never find truth, because he is never free. Being, which is recognizing what is, accepting and living with what is—not trying to transform it, not condemning it—brings about virtue, and in that there is freedom. Only when the mind is not cultivating memory, when it is not seeking righteousness as a means of resistance, is there freedom, and in that freedom there comes reality, the bliss of which must be experienced.

❖

Question: You don't seem to think that we in India have won our independence. According to you, what would be the state of real freedom?

Krishnamurti: Sir, freedom becomes isolation when it is nationalistic, and isolation inevitably leads to conflict, because nothing can exist in isolation. To be is to be related, and merely to isolate yourself within a national frontier invites confusion, sorrow, starvation, conflict, war—which has been proved over and over again. So independence as a State apart inevitably leads to conflict and to war, because independence for most of us implies isolation. And when you have isolated yourself as a national entity, have you gained freedom? Have you gained freedom from exploitation, from class struggle, from starvation, from conflicting religiosity, from the priest, from communal strife, from leadership? Obviously you have not. You have only driven out the white exploiter, and the brown has taken his place—probably a little more ruthlessly. We have the same thing as before, the same exploitation, the same priests, the same organized religion, the same superstitions, and class wars. And has that given us freedom? Sir, we don't want to be free. Don't let us fool ourselves. Because freedom implies intelligence, love; freedom implies non-exploitation, non-submission to authority; freedom implies extraordinary virtue. As I said, righteousness is always an isolating process, for isolation and righteousness go together; whereas virtue and freedom are co-existent. A sovereign nation is always isolated, and therefore can never be free; it is a cause of constant strife, of suspicion, antagonism, and war.

Surely freedom must begin with the individual, who is a total process, not antagonistic to the mass. The individual is the total process of the world, and if he merely isolates himself in nationalism or in righteousness, then he is the cause of disaster and misery. But if the individual—who is a total process, not opposed to the mass, but who is a result of the mass, of the whole—if the individual transforms himself, his life, then for him there is freedom. And because he is the result of a total process, when he liberates himself from nationalism, from greed, from exploitation, he has direct action upon the whole. The regeneration of the individual is not in the future but now, and if you postpone your regeneration to tomorrow, you are inviting confusion, you are caught in the wave of darkness. Regeneration is now, not tomorrow, because understanding is only in the present. You don't understand now because you don't give your heart and mind, your whole attention, to that which you want to understand. If you give your mind and heart to understand, you will have understanding. Sir, if you give your mind and your heart to find out the cause of violence, if you are fully aware of it, you will be non-violent now. But unfortunately, you have so conditioned your mind by religious postponement and social ethics that you are incapable of looking at it directly—and that is our trouble.

So understanding is always in the present and never in the future. Understanding is now, not in the days to come. And freedom, which is not isolation, can come into being only when each one of us understands his responsibility to the whole. The individual is the product of the whole—he is not a separate process, he is the result of the whole. After all, you are the result of all India, of all humanity. You may call yourself by whatever name you like, but you are the result of a total process, which is man. And if you, the psychological you, are not free, how can you have freedom outwardly; of what significance is external freedom? You may have different governments—and good god, is that freedom? You may have the multiplication of provinces, because each person wants a job, but is that freedom? Sir, we are fed by words without much content; we darken the councils with words that have no meaning; we have fed on propaganda, which is a lie. We have not thought out these problems for ourselves, because most of us want to be led. We don't want to think and find out, because to think is very painful, very disillusioning. Either we think and become disillusioned and cynical—or we think and go beyond. When you go beyond and above all thought process, then there is freedom. And in that there is joy, in that there is creative being, which a righteous man, an isolated man, can never understand.

SO OUR PROBLEM is that our thoughts wander all over the place, and naturally we want to bring about order. But how is order to be brought about? Now, to understand a fast revolving machine, you must slow it down, must you not? If you want to understand a dynamo, it must be slowed down and studied, but if you stop it, it is a dead thing, and a dead thing can never be understood. Only a living thing can be understood. So a mind that has killed thoughts by exclusion, by isolation, can have no understanding, but the mind can understand thought if the thought process is slowed down. If you have seen a slow motion picture, you will understand the marvellous movement of a horse's muscles as it jumps. There is beauty in that slow movement of the muscles, but as the horse jumps hurriedly, as the movement is quickly over, that beauty is lost. Similarly, when the mind moves slowly because it wants to understand each thought as it arises, then there is freedom from thinking, freedom from controlled, disciplined thought. Thinking is the response of memory, therefore thinking can never be creative. Only in meeting the new as the new, the fresh as the fresh, is there creative being. The mind is the recorder, the gatherer of memories, and as long as memory is being revivified by challenge, the thought process must go on. But if each thought is observed, felt out, gone into fully, and completely understood, then you will find that memory begins to wither away. We are talking about psychological memory, not factual memory.

Bangalore, 18 July 1948

WHAT WE ARE trying to discuss and find out is whether life has a purpose, and whether that purpose can be measured. It can only be measured in terms of the known, in terms of the past, and when I measure the purpose of life in terms of the known, I will measure it according to my likes and dislikes. Therefore, the purpose will be conditioned by my desires, and therefore it ceases to be the purpose. Surely that is clear, is it not? I can understand what is the purpose of life only through the screen of my own prejudices, wants, and desires—otherwise I cannot judge, can I? So, the measure, the tape, the yardstick, is a conditioning of my mind, and according to the dictates of my conditioning I will decide what the purpose is. But *is* that the purpose of life? It is created by my want, and therefore it is surely not the purpose of life. To find out the purpose of life, the mind must be free of measurement; then only can it find out. Otherwise you are merely projecting your own want. This is not mere intellectualization, and if you go into it deeply you will see its significance. After all, it is according to my prejudice, to my want, to my desire, to my predilection, that I decide what the purpose of life is to be. So my desire creates the purpose. Surely that is not the purpose of life. Which is more important, to find out the purpose of life, or to free the mind itself from its own conditioning? And when the mind is free from its own conditioning, that very freedom itself is the purpose. Because, after all, it is only in freedom that one can discover any truth.

So the first requisite is freedom, not seeking the purpose of life. Without freedom, obviously, one cannot find it; without being liberated from our own petty little wants, pursuits, ambitions, envies, and ill will, without freedom from these things, how can one possibly inquire or discover what is the purpose of life? So, is it not important, for one who is inquiring about the purpose of life, to find out first if the instrument of inquiry is capable of penetrating into the processes of life, into the psychological complexities of one's own being? Because, that is all we have, is it not?—a psychological instrument that is shaped to suit our own needs. And as the instrument is fashioned out of our own petty desires, as it is the outcome of our own experiences, worries, anxieties, and ill will, how can such an instrument find reality? Therefore, is it not important, if you are to inquire into the purpose of life, to find out first if the inquirer is capable of understanding or discovering what that purpose is? I am not turning the tables on you, but that is what is implied when we inquire about the purpose of life. When we ask that question, we have first to find out whether the questioner, the inquirer, is capable of understanding.

Poona, 31 January 1953

Question: Even after the end of the British rule, there is no radical change in the system of our education. The stress as well as the demand is for specialization: technical and professional training. How best can education become the means to the realization of true freedom?

Krishnamurti: Sir, what do we mean by true freedom? Political freedom? Or is it freedom to think what you like? Can you think what you like? And does thinking bring about freedom? Is not all thinking conditioned thinking? So what do we mean by true freedom?

So far as we know, education is conditioned thinking, is it not? All that we are concerned with is to acquire a job or use that knowledge for self-satisfaction, for self-aggrandizement, to get on in the world. Is it not important to see what we mean by true freedom? Perhaps if we understand that, then the training in some technique for professional specialization may have its value. But merely to cultivate technical capacity without understanding what is true freedom leads to destruction, to greater wars, and that is actually what is happening in the world now. So let us find out what we mean by true freedom.

Obviously the first necessity for freedom is that there should be no fear—not only the fear imposed by society but also the psychological fear of insecurity. You may have a very good job, and you may be climbing up the ladder of success, but if there is ambition, if there is the struggle to be somebody, does that not entail fear? And does that not imply that he who is very successful is not truly free? So fear imposed by tradition, by the so-called responsibility of the edicts of society, or your own fear of death, of insecurity, of disease—all this prevents the true freedom of being, does it not?

So freedom is not possible if there is any form of outward or inward compulsion. Compulsion comes into being when there is the urge to conform to the pattern of society, or to the pattern that you have created for yourself, as being good or not good. The pattern is created by thought, which is the outcome of the past, of your tradition, of your education, of your whole experience based on the past. So as long as there is any form of compulsion—governmental, religious, or your own pattern that you have created for yourself through your desire to fulfil, to become great—there will be no true freedom. It is not an easy thing to do, nor is it an easy thing to understand what we mean by true freedom. But we can see that as long as there is fear in any form we cannot know what true freedom is.

Individually or collectively, if there is fear, compulsion, there can be no freedom. We may speculate about true freedom, but actual freedom is different from speculative ideas about freedom.

So as long as the mind is seeking any form of security— and that is what most of us want—as long as the mind is seeking permanency in any form, there can be no freedom. As long as individually or collectively we seek security, there must be war, which is an obvious fact, and that is what is happening in the world today. So there can be true freedom only when the mind understands this whole process of the desire for security, for permanency. After all, that is what you want in your gods, in your gurus. In your social relationships, your governments, you want security; so you invest your god with the ultimate security, which is above you; you clothe that image with the idea that you as an entity are such a transient being, and that there at least you have permanency. So you begin with the desire to be religiously permanent, and all your political, religious, and social activities, whatever they are, are based on that desire for permanency—to be certain, to perpetuate yourselves through the family or through the nation or through an idea, through your son. How can such a mind that is seeking constantly, consciously or unconsciously, permanency, security, how can such a mind ever have freedom?

We really do not seek true freedom. We seek something different from freedom; we seek better conditions, a better state. We do not want freedom; we want better, superior, nobler conditions, and that we call education. Can this education produce peace in the world? Certainly not. On the contrary, it is going to produce greater wars and misery. As long as you are a Hindu, Moslem, or god knows what else, you are going to create strife—for yourself, for your neighbour and nation. Do we realize this? Look at what is happening! I do not have to tell you because you already know it.

Instead of being integrated human beings, you are thinking separatively; your activities are fractioned, broken up, disintegrated—you are all fighting. That is the result of this so-called freedom and so-called education. You say that you have unity religiously, but actually you are fighting, destroying each other, because you do not see the whole process of living, because you are only concerned with tomorrow or to have better jobs. You will go out after listening and do exactly the same thing. You will be a sectarian forgetting the rest of the world. As long as you are thinking in those terms you are going to have wars, miseries, destruction. You will never be safe, neither you nor your children, though you want to be safe, and therefore you are thinking in this narrow regional way. As long as you have these ways, you have got to have wars.

Your present way of living indicates that you really do not want to have freedom; what you want is merely a better way of living, more safety, more contentment, to be assured of a job, to be assured of your position, religiously, politically. Such people cannot create a new world. They are not religious people. They are not intelligent people. They are thinking in terms of immediate results like all politicians. And you know that as long as you leave the world to politicians, you are going to have destruction, wars, misery. Sirs, please don't smile. It is your responsibility, not your leaders' responsibility; it is your own individual responsibility.

Freedom is something entirely different. Freedom comes into being; it cannot be sought after. It comes into being when there is no fear, when there is love in your heart. You cannot have love and think in terms of a Hindu, a Christian, a Moslem, a Parsi. Freedom comes into being only when the mind is no longer seeking security for itself, either in tradition or in knowledge. A mind that is crippled with knowledge or burdened with knowledge is not a free mind. The mind is only free when it is capable of meeting life at every moment, meeting the reality that every incident, that every thought, that every experience reveals. And that revelation is not possible when the mind is crippled by the past.

It is the responsibility of the educator to create a new human being, to bring about a different human being, fearless, self-reliant, who will create his own society—a society totally unlike ours, because ours is based on fear, envy, ambition, corruption. True freedom can only come when intelligence comes into being—that is, the understanding of the whole, the total process of existence.

Bombay, 8 March 1953

Question: You have been talking of freedom. Does not freedom demand duties? What is my duty to society, to myself?

Krishnamurti: Are freedom and duty comparable? Can the dutiful son be free? Can I be dutiful to society and yet be free? Can I be dutiful and yet be revolutionary in the right sense, not in the economic sense? Can I, if I follow a system, political or religious, ever be free? Or do I merely imitate, copy? Is not this whole system imitation? Being a dutiful son, doing what my father wants me to do, doing the right thing according to society—do these not themselves connote a feeling of imitation? My father wants me to be a lawyer; is it my duty to become a lawyer? My father says I must join some religious organization; is it my duty to do so?

Does duty go with love? It is only when there is no love, when there is no freedom, that the word "duty" becomes extraordinarily important. And duty then takes the place of tradition. In that state we live, that is our state, is it not?—I must be dutiful.

What is my duty to society? What is my duty to myself? Sirs, society demands a great many things of you: you must obey, you must follow, you must do certain ceremonies, perform certain rituals, believe. It conditions you to certain forms of thought, to certain beliefs. If you are finding what is real—not what is dutiful to society, not trying to conform to a particular pattern—if you are trying to find out what is truth, must you not be free?

Being free does not mean that you must throw something aside, that you must be antagonistic to everything: that is not freedom. Freedom implies constant awareness of thought; it implies that which is unfolding the implications of duty, and out of which—but not by merely throwing aside a particular freedom—freedom comes. You cannot understand all traditions, you cannot grasp the full significance of them if you condemn or justify or identify yourself with a particular thought or an idea. When I begin to inquire what is my duty to myself or to society, how shall I find out? What is the criterion? What is the standard? Or, shall we find out why we depend on these words? How quickly the mind that is searching, seeking, inquiring, is gripped by the word duty! The aging father says to his son, "It is your duty to support me," and the son feels it his duty to support him. And though he may want to do something else, to paint pictures, which will not give him the means of livelihood to support his father and himself, he says his duty is to earn and to put aside what he really wants to do, and for the rest of his life he is caught. For the rest of his life he is bitter; he has bitterness in his heart and he gives money to his father and mother. That is our life, we live in bitterness and we die with bitterness.

Because we really have no love and because we have no freedom, we use words to control our thoughts, to shape our hearts and feelings, and we are satisfied. Surely love may be the only way of revolution, and it *is* the only way. But most of us object to revolutions, not only the superficial, the economic revolutions, but the more essential, the deeper, the more significant revolution of thought, the revolution of creation. Since we object to that, we are always reforming on top, patching up here and there with words, with threats, with ambitions.

You will say, at the end of this, that I have not answered your question, "What is my duty to society, to my father and to myself." I say that is a wrong question. It is a question put by a mind that is not free, a mind that is not in revolt, a mind that is docile, submissive, a mind that has no love. Can such a mind that is docile, submissive, without love, with that shadow of bitterness, ever be dutiful to society or to itself? Can such a mind create a new world, a new structure?

Do not shake your heads. Do you know what you want? You do not want a revolt, you do not want a revolution of the mind, you want to bring up your children in the same manner in which you have been brought up. You want to condition them the same way, to think on the same lines, to attend religious rituals, to believe what you believe. So you never encourage them to find out. As you are destroying yourselves in your conditioning, you want to destroy others. So the problem is not "What is my duty to society?" but "How do I find or awaken this love and this freedom?" When once there is that love, you may not be dutiful at all.

Love is the most revolutionary thing, but the mind cannot conceive that love. You cannot cultivate it, it must be there; it is not a thing to be grown in your backyard; it is a thing that comes into being with constant inquiry, constant discontent and revolt, when you never follow authority, when you are without fear—which means, when you have the capacity to make mistakes and from those mistakes to find out the answer. A mind that is without fear is really not petty, and it is capable of real depth; then such a mind shall find out what love is, what freedom is.

With Children at Rajghat School, Varanasi, 20 January 1954

Question: What is freedom?

Krishnamurti: I wonder if she really wants to know what freedom is! Do any of us know what freedom is? All that we know is we are made to do things, we are compelled by circumstances or through our own fears to do things, and we want to break away from them. The breaking away from restraint, from compulsion, from fear, or something else is what we call freedom. Please listen.

The breaking away from restraint, the breaking away from a hindrance, the breaking away from some form of compulsion is not freedom. Freedom is something in itself, not away from something. Understand this, please. The prisoner put in a prison for some cause wants to break away and be free. He only thinks in terms of breaking away. If I am angry, I feel that if I can only break away from anger, I will be free. If I am envious, the overcoming of the envy is not freedom; the breaking away, the overcoming, the suppressing is merely another kind of expressing the same thing; that is not freedom. Freedom is in itself, not away from anything. The love of something for itself is freedom. There is freedom when you paint because you love to paint, not because it gives you fame or gives you a position. In the school, when you love to paint, that very love is freedom, and that means an astonishing understanding of all the ways of the mind. Also, it is very simple to do something for itself and not for what it brings you either as a punishment or as a reward. Just to love the thing for itself is the beginning of freedom.

Do you spend ten minutes of your class period talking of all this? Or do you plunge immediately into geography, mathematics, and English and all the rest of it? What happens? Why don't you do this for ten minutes every day instead of wasting your time on some stupid stuff that does not really interest you but that has to be done. Why don't you spend some time with the teacher in the class, and talk about these matters? This will help you in your life though it might not help you to become great or successful or famous. If you talk over these matters every day for ten minutes, intelligently, fearlessly, then it will help you all through life, because it will make you think and not merely repeat things like parrots. So please ask your teachers to talk to you about these matters. Then you will find both the educator and yourself becoming more intelligent.

Poona, 21 September 1958

SURELY THERE ARE several kinds of freedom: there is political freedom; there is the freedom that knowledge gives, when you know how to do things, the know-how; the freedom of a wealthy man who can go around the world; the freedom of capacity, to be able to write, to express oneself, to think clearly. Then there is the freedom from something: freedom from oppression, freedom from envy, freedom from tradition, from ambition, and so on. And then there is the freedom that is gained, we hope, at the end—at the end of a discipline, at the end of acquiring virtue, at the end of effort—the ultimate freedom we hope to get through doing certain things. So the freedom that capacity gives, the freedom from something and the freedom we are supposed to gain at the end of a virtuous life—those are types of freedom we all know. Now are not those various freedoms merely reactions? When you say: "I want to be free from anger," that is merely a reaction; it is not freedom from anger. And the freedom that you think you will get at the end of a virtuous life, by struggle, by discipline, that is also a reaction to what has been. Please follow this carefully, because I am going to say something somewhat difficult in the sense that you are not accustomed to it. There is a sense of freedom that is not *from* anything, that has no cause, but that is a state of being free. You see, the freedom that we know is always brought about by will, is it not? I will be free; I will learn a technique; I will become a specialist; I will study—and that will give me freedom. So we use will as a means of achieving freedom, do we not? I do not want to be poor and therefore I exercise my capacity, my will, everything to get rich. Or I am vain and I exercise will not to be vain. So we think we shall get freedom through the exercise of will. But will does not bring freedom, on the contrary.

❖

As I HAVE been pointing out, freedom from something is not freedom. You are trying to be free from anger; I do not say you must not be free from anger, but I say that is not freedom. I may be rid of greed, pettiness, envy, or a dozen other things and yet not be free. Freedom is a quality of the mind. That quality does not come about through very careful, respectable searchings and inquiries, through very careful analysis or putting ideas together. That is why it is important to see the truth that the freedom we are constantly demanding is always from something, such as freedom from sorrow. Not that there is no freedom from sorrow, but the demand to be free from it is merely a reaction and therefore does not free you from sorrow. Am I making myself clear? I am in sorrow for various reasons, and I say I must be free. The urge to be free of sorrow is born out of pain. I suffer, because of my husband, or my son, or something else; I do not like that state I am in and I want to get away from it. That desire for freedom is a reaction, it is not freedom. It is just another desirable state I want in opposition to what is. The man who can travel around the world because he has plenty of money is not necessarily free, nor is the man who is clever or efficient, for his wanting to be free is again merely a reaction. So can I not see that freedom, liberation, cannot be learned or acquired or sought after through any reaction? Therefore I must understand the reaction, and I must also understand that freedom does not come through any effort of will. Will and freedom are contradictory, as thought and freedom are contradictory. Thought cannot produce freedom because thought is conditioned. Economically you can, perhaps, arrange the world so that man can be more comfortable, have more food, clothing, and shelter, and you may think that is freedom. Those are necessary and essential things, but that is not the totality of freedom. Freedom is a state and quality of mind. And it is that quality we are inquiring into. Without that quality, do what you will, cultivate all the virtues in the world, you will not have that freedom.

Bombay, 3 December 1958

IN ALL FORMS of communication words, naturally, are very important. They become more so when you are dealing with abstract and rather complicated problems because each one will translate every word according to his own understanding of it. So it is very difficult when one wants to deal with the extraordinary problem of life, with all its complexities and subtleties. Words become really significant if we can keep to their dictionary meaning and also allow ourselves to go beyond the mere definition, beyond any mere conclusion that a word may convey.

Take for example the word *freedom*. Each one will translate it according to his own particular necessity, demand, pressures, and fears. If you are an ambitious man you will translate that word as something necessary in order to carry out your ambitions, fulfil your desires. To a man who is bound to certain traditions, freedom is a word to be afraid of. To a man who indulges himself in all his fancies and desires that word conveys the possibility of further indulgence. So words have an extraordinary significance in our life and I do not know if you have ever realized how deep and profound the significance of the word is. The words *god, freedom, Communist, American, Hindu, Christian,* and so on, influence us not only neurologically but they verbally vibrate in our being, bringing out certain reactions. I do not know if you realize all this and, if you do realize it, you will know that it is very difficult to free the mind from the word. As I want to talk over with you a very complex problem, I think we should come to it with the hesitancy and the clarification of a mind that not only understands the words and their significance but that is capable also of going beyond the word.

One can see what is happening throughout the world at the present time. Wherever there are tyrannies, freedom is denied; wherever there is the powerful organization of the church, of religion, freedom again is denied. Though they use this word *freedom*, both the religious and the political organizations refuse that freedom. Also one can see that where there is overpopulation freedom must inevitably decline, and wherever there is over-organization, mass communication, freedom is denied. So seeing all this, how is an individual like you or me to interpret freedom? Living, as one has to in this world, in a society that is completely bound to organizations, in which technicians are very important, the mind becomes a slave to a certain form of technique, to a method, to certain ways. So at what level, at what depth do we translate that word *freedom?* If you walked out of your office that would not mean freedom, you would merely lose your job. If you drove on the wrong side of the road, the policeman would be after you and your freedom would be curtailed. If you do what you like, or if you get rich, the State will control you. All around us there are sanctions, laws, traditions, various forms of compulsion and domination, and all these are preventing freedom.

So if, as a human being, you would understand this problem, which is a real problem, then from what depth are you inquiring? Or are you not concerned at all? I am afraid most of us are not concerned; what we are concerned with is our daily bread, our families, our little troubles, jealousies, ambitions, but we are not concerned with the wider, bigger problems. And the mere concern for the solution of the problem will not produce a remedy. You might find an immediate remedy, but that will only produce other problems, as one well knows. So at what level, from what depth do you respond to the word *freedom?*

One must also realize, surely, that the word is not the thing. The word *truth* is not the truth. But for most of us the word is sufficient; we do not go beyond the word and investigate what lies behind the word. Do please consider this. The very word *Moslem* prevents you from looking at the human being who represents that word. The nervous response and the psychological response to that word are very deep, and it evokes in you all kinds of ideas, beliefs, prejudices. But if one could think very deeply, it would become obvious that one must separate the word from the actual thing. A great deal of misunderstanding in our relationships lies in the wrong significance we give to words. Therefore it is very important that you and I, as two individuals, establish right communication so that we understand each other on the same level at the same time. I do not know if you have noticed it, but when you love somebody communication between the two of you is immediate. Similarly, if we can establish such communion then I think we shall be able to explore this very complex problem. The great difficulty in establishing communication is the word, and you and I must pierce through the word and go beyond if we are to commune with each other, to share, partake in the problem that we are going to unroll, uncover, discuss.

❖

WE SEE THAT the process of thinking is the response of memory, which is acting all the time like a machine. So one asks: "What does freedom mean?" I hope you understand this question and that I am making myself clear. If my whole mind is the result of time, the result of tradition, of various cultures, experiences, conditionings, of having the background of my family, the race, the belief, of always functioning within the field of the known—then where is freedom? If I am moving, as I am, all the time within the limits of my own mind, which is full of memories and the product of time, how is the mind to go beyond itself? The word *freedom* to such a mind means nothing—does it?—because it only turns freedom into another demand, saying: "How can I be free?" Please follow this carefully and you will see. I realize, consciously or unconsciously, that mine is a very narrow life; there is perpetual anxiety, struggle, fear, misery, sorrow, and so on, and so I say, I must be free; I must have peace of mind; I must escape from this limitation. This is what each one of us is demanding. Outwardly, under the various tyrannical governments, there is no freedom—you are told what to do and you do it—and inwardly the same problem continues. Here, in a so-called democratic country you are more or less outwardly free—more or less—but inwardly you are a prisoner, and you are asking this question about freedom. The greater the organization of a church or of a society, and the greater the efficiency and the means of mass communication, the greater is the conflict and turmoil. So we are always in a struggle with our environment and within ourselves. Struggle is going on perpetually and there is contradiction and misery: "My wife does not love me." "I love someone else." "There is death." "I believe, I do not believe." There is ever turmoil and restlessness, as with the sea.

Have you ever watched the sea? There are certain days when the wind is quiet, there is no breath of air, and the sea reflects the stars. There is a tranquillity, a breathlessness, a sense of peace, but beneath there are deep currents, deep movements; its waters cover an enormous area and actually it is never still, it is ever moving, moving restlessly. Every breath that comes shatters the quietness, the stillness. So also is the mind. We are eternally restless, and becoming aware of that we say: "Give me peace. Let me find god. I want to escape from this misery and to find out if there is an everlasting peace, bliss." That is all we want, and that is why we are in such a frightful struggle, such a tension of contradiction, one desire battling against another. Ambition breeds frustration and emptiness, and then this desire to fulfil again brings the shadow of frustration. It is no use my merely describing our state—we are aware of it, are we not?—from the state of confusion, turmoil, misery, grief, to the state of a sense of passing joys, of occasionally looking at the sky and saying: "How beautiful, how wonderful!"

and occasionally knowing the feeling of love. But it is all temporary, fleeting, it is all in a flux. So the mind says: "Is there not a permanent state of peace?" and it proceeds to invest an idea of god, of
Truth, with permanence. And all the religions encourage this
investiture of an idea with permanency. Every religion in the world
says that there is a permanency, a bliss that you must seek and that
there is a way to it. They say there is a path from turmoil to reality.
You understand, sir? The moment you are seeking a state that will
be permanent, you must find a way to it: a belief, a method, a system, a practice. Now to me there is neither a permanency nor a
method. There is no method to discover reality.

Bombay, 14 December 1958

THINKING, SURELY, IS superficial; it is the response of memory—the collected experiences, the conditioning—and according to that conditioning, which is our background, thought responds to any challenge. Thought is always bound to this collected experience, and the question is: Can thinking ever be free? Because it is only in freedom that one can observe, it is only in freedom that one can discover, it is only in a state of spontaneity, where there is no compulsion, no immediate demand, no pressure of social influence, that real discovery is possible. Surely, to observe what you are thinking, why you think, and the source and motive of your thought, there must be a certain sense of spontaneity, of freedom, because any influence whatsoever gives a twist to observation. With all thinking, if there is any compulsion or pressure, thought becomes crooked. So can thought ever set man free, set the mind free, and is freedom the essential necessity if one is to discover what is true? There are two usual different types of freedom: there is the freedom from something or the freedom to fulfil, to be something. Then there is also freedom, just freedom. Most of us just want to be free from something—free from time or free from a relative, or else we want to be free to be fulfilled, to express ourselves. All our ideas of freedom are limited to those two—the freedom from something or the freedom to be something. Now both are reactions, are they not? Both are the result of thought, the outcome of some form of inward or outward compulsion. Thought is caught in that process; thought seeks freedom from tyranny, freedom from a corrupt government, freedom from a particular relationship, freedom from a feeling of anxiety, and in freeing oneself, one hopes to be able to fulfil oneself in something else. So we always think in terms of freedom from, or freedom to be, to fulfil. And it seems to be that thinking of freedom only in those two categories is very superficial.

So is there a freedom that is not merely a reaction, in which there is neither a movement from nor a movement to be? And can such a freedom be captured, engendered as an idea by thought? Because if you are merely free from something you are not really free, and if you are free in the sense of being fulfilled, there is always anxiety, fear, frustration, and sorrow. Can thought free the mind so that sorrow and anxiety have ceased altogether? Surely, as with love, real goodness is not cultivated by thought; it is a state of being, but that state cannot be brought about by the mind that says to itself, "I must be good." So can one find out, by searching through the various channels of thought, what freedom is? Can thought uncover the true significance of life, unfold reality? Or must thought be totally suspended for reality to be?

Let me put it differently. You are seeking something, are you not? If you are a so-called religious person you are seeking what you call god, or else you are seeking more money, more happiness, or you want to be good; you are seeking the expression of your ambition. Everyone is seeking something.

Now what do we mean by seeking? To seek implies that you know what it is you are seeking. When you say you are seeking peace of mind, it must mean either that you have already experienced it and want it back, or you are projecting a verbal idea that is not an actuality but a thing created by thought. So search implies that you have already known or experienced what you seek. You cannot seek something that you do not know. When you say you are seeking god, it means you already know what god is or else your conditioning has projected the idea that there is a god. So thinking compels you to seek that which thought itself has projected.

Thought, which is superficial, thought, the result of many experiences that have been gathered and that form your background—from that thought you project an idea and then you seek it! And in your search for god you have visions, you have experiences that only strengthen the search and urge you on to follow the projections of your background. So searching is still the motion of thought. One is in conflict, in turmoil, and in order to escape from that turmoil thought begins to project an idea that there must be peace, that there must be permanent bliss, and then it proceeds to seek it. This is actually what is taking place in each one of us. One does not understand this miserable existence, this everlasting chaos, and one wants to escape to a permanent state of bliss. Now that state is projected by the mind, and having projected it thought says: "I must find help to get to it." And so follow the methods, the system, the practice. Thought creates the problem and then tries to escape from the problem through various systems in order to reach the projected idea of a permanent state. So thought pursues its own projection, its own shadow. Now, the question is, really: Can the mind suspend thinking and face everyday experience from a different quality of mind? This does not mean to forget or neglect collected memory, collected experience. Technicians, bridge-builders, scientists, clerks, and so on are, of course, needed, but is it possible, realizing that thinking is not the solution to our problems, to suspend thought and observe the problem? I do not know if you have ever tried really to look at a problem without the agitation, the turmoil, the restlessness of thought. Thinking creates a series of motions of restlessness, of anxiety, of demand for a solution. Have you ever tried to sink thought, to suspend thinking and just observe the problem? Please try it, as I am talking. Listen so that you can look at the problem without the agitation of thought.

You have many problems—problems of relationship, of family, problems of your work, your responsibilities, problems of your social, environmental, or political life—whether they are immediate, pressing, or remote. Take any one of those problems and look at it. You have always looked at it—have you not?—with a certain agitation of thought that says: "I must solve it; what am I to do; is this right or is that; is this respectable or not possible?" and so on and on. And with this restless thought you examine the problem, and obviously whatever solution you find through that restlessness is not a true answer and only creates more problems. That is what is actually taking place with each one of us. So can you look at the problem suspending your thought? Thought is the result of collected experiences and those memories respond to the problem, but can you suspend thought so that for the moment your mind is not under pressure, not under the weight of a thousand yesterdays? It is not merely a matter of saying: "I will not think." That is impossible. But if you see the truth that an agitated mind that is merely responding according to its conditioning, its background, its accumulated experiences cannot resolve or understand the problem—if you see the truth of that fact totally, then you understand that thought is not the instrument that will resolve our problems.

Let me put it differently. It seems that whatever man can do, an appropriate electronic machine can do also. It is being discovered, and will be perfected in a decade or two, that what a human mind can do, the machine can do also and quite efficiently. It will probably compose, write poems, translate books, and so on. And chemically they are making drugs to give comfort, peace, freedom from worry, tranquillization. So you understand what is going to happen? Is the machine to take over your work and probably do it better, and is the drug to give you peace of mind? Suppose there are certain drugs you can take to make your mind extraordinarily quiet so that you won't have to go through disciplines, controls, breathing exercises, and all those tricks. So the petty mind, the shallow mind, the limited mind that only thinks an inch from itself, will have no more worries, it will have peace. But such a mind is still petty, its frontiers are recognizable and all its thoughts are shallow. Though it is very quiet through taking pills, it has not broken down its own limitations, has it? A petty mind thinking about god, going from one graven image to another, uttering a lot of words, murmuring a lot of prayers, is still a petty mind. And that is the case with most of us. So how can thought, which is always superficial, always petty, always limited, how can that thought be suspended so that there is no frontier at all, so that there is freedom—but not the freedom from something or the freedom to be something? I hope you understand the question.

You see, one can forever improve oneself—one can think a little more, apply oneself to self-improvement, be more kind, more generous, this or that, but it is always within the field of the self, the "me." It is the "me" that is achieving, becoming, and that "me" is always recognizable as a collection of experiences, memories. And the problem is how to resolve, to break down, the frontiers of the "me." When I say "how," I do not imply a method but an inquiry. Because all methods involve the functioning of thought, the control of thought, the substitution of one thought for another. So when you merely have methods, systems, disciplines, there is no inquiry.

Seeing all this, that thought is the result of memory, of collected experience, which is very limited, and that the seeking of reality, god, truth, perfection, beauty is really the projection of thought—in conflict with the present and going toward an idea of the future—and seeing that the pursuit of the future creates time, seeing all this, surely it is obvious that thought must be suspended. There must be something, surely, that thought cannot capture and put into memory, something totally new, completely unknowable, unrecognizable. And how are you, with the restlessness of your thought, to understand that state?

Is understanding a matter of time? Will you understand this tomorrow, by thinking about it? You know how, if you have a problem, thought investigates it, analyzes it, tears it to pieces, goes into it as much as it can, and still has no answer, because it is always with the anxiety of the problem. Then it gives it up, lays it in abeyance, and because thought has dissociated itself from the problem so that the problem is no longer pressing on the mind, consciously or unconsciously, then the answer comes. It must have happened to you.

So can we not see through this whole business of thinking? You know how you worship the intellectual man who is full of knowledge, which is nothing but words and ideas, but who is still living on the superficial level. Have you observed how instinctively you are attracted to a man who says, "I know"? So, seeing all this, the question is, can thought be suspended? If you have understood the problem, then as I begin to explore it further, you will be able to follow.

❖

THERE IS THE problem of death, the problem of god, of virtue, of relationship; there is the problem of the conflict we are in, the job, the lack of money; there is the problem of poverty, starvation, and the whole misery of despair and hope. You cannot solve these problems one by one; it is impossible. You have to solve them totally, as a whole thing, not little by little; otherwise you will never solve them. Because in solving one problem as though it were dissociated from the others you merely create another problem. No problem is separate, isolated. Every problem is related to another problem, superficially or deeply, so you have to comprehend it totally. And thought can never comprehend it totally because thought is partial, is fragmentary. So how is the mind to solve the problem? You cannot solve it as though it were isolated; you cannot find a solution through an intellectual abstraction; you cannot solve it through accumulated memories; you cannot solve it by escaping to the temple, or to alcohol, or to sex or anything else. It must be comprehended totally, understood totally, and this can happen only when there is the suspension of thought. When the mind is motionless and still, the reflection of the problem on the mind is entirely different. When the lake is very quiet you can see the depth of it, you can see every fish, every weed, every flutter; similarly, when the mind is completely motionless one can see very, very clearly. This can only take place when there is a suspension of thought, not in order to resolve the problem, but to see its significance, its fragmentary nature; and then thought of itself becomes quiet, motionless, not only at the conscious level but profoundly.

That is why self-knowledge is essential, why it is essential to learn about yourself. And you cannot learn about yourself if you do not look, or if you look with a mind that is full of accumulated knowledge. To learn, you must be free. Then you can look at the problem not merely from the surface; then every issue, every challenge is responded to from a depth that thought cannot reach.

A motionless mind, a still mind, is not decayed, dead, corrupt as is the mind that has been made still by a drug, by breathing, or by any system of self-hypnosis. It is a mind that is fully alive; every untrodden region of itself is lighted up, and from that centre of light it responds—and it does not create a shadow.

Madras, 22 November 1959

I WONDER IF you are at all aware of this extraordinary compulsion to belong to something? I am sure most of you belong to some political party, to a certain group or organized belief; you are committed to a particular way of thinking or living, and that surely denies freedom. I do not know if you have examined this compulsion to belong, to identify oneself with a country, with a system, with a group, with certain political or religious beliefs. And obviously, without understanding this compulsion to belong, merely to walk out of one party or group has no meaning, because you will soon commit yourself to another.

Have you not done this very thing? Leaving one "ism," you go and join something else—Catholicism, Communism, Moral Rearmament, and god knows what else. You move from one commitment to another, compelled by the urge to belong to something. Why? I think it is an important question to ask oneself. Why do you want to belong? Surely it is only when the mind stands completely alone that it is capable of receiving what is true—not when it has committed itself to some party or belief. Please do think about this question, commune with it in your heart. Why do you belong? Why have you committed yourself to a country, to a party, to an ideology, to a belief, to a family, to a race? Why is there this desire to identify yourself with something? And what are the implications of this commitment? It is only the man who is completely outside who can understand—not the man who is pledged to a particular group, or who is perpetually moving from one group to another, from one commitment to another.

Surely, you want to belong to something because it gives you a sense of security—not only social security, but also inward security. When you belong to something, you feel safe. By belonging to this thing called Hinduism, you feel socially respectable, inwardly safe, secure. So you have committed yourself to something in order to feel safe, secure—which obviously narrows down the margin of freedom, does it not?

Most of us are not free. We are slaves to Hinduism, to Communism, to one society or another, to leaders, to political parties, to organized religions, to gurus, and so we have lost our dignity as human beings. There is dignity as a human being only when one has tasted, smelled, known this extraordinary thing called freedom. Out of the flowering of freedom comes human dignity. But if we do not know this freedom, we are enslaved. That is what is happening in the world, is it not? And I think the desire to belong, to commit ourselves to something, is one of the causes of this narrowing down of freedom. To be rid of this urge to belong, to be free of the desire to commit oneself, one has to inquire into one's own way of thinking, to commune with oneself, with one's own heart and desires. That is a very difficult thing to do. It requires patience, a certain tenderness of approach, a constant and persistent searching into oneself without condemnation or acceptance. That is true meditation, but you will find it is not easy to do, and very few of us are willing to undertake it.

Most of us choose the easy path of being guided, being led; we belong to something, and thereby lose our human dignity. Probably you will say, "Well, I have heard this before, he is on his favourite subject," and go away. I wish it were possible for you to listen as if you were listening for the first time—like seeing the sunset, or the face of your friend for the first time. Then you would learn, and thus learning, you would discover freedom for yourself—which is not the so-called freedom offered by another.

So let us inquire patiently and persistently into this question of what is freedom. Surely only a free man can comprehend the truth, which is to find out if there is an eternal something beyond the measure of the mind, and the man who is burdened with his own experience or knowledge is never free, because knowledge prevents learning.

We are going to commune with each other, to inquire together into this question of what is freedom, and how to come by it. And thus to inquire, there must obviously be freedom right from the start, otherwise you cannot inquire, can you? You must totally cease to belong, for only then is your mind capable of inquiring. But if your mind is tethered, held by some commitment, whether political, religious, social, or economic, then that very commitment will prevent you from inquiring, because for you there is no freedom.

Do please listen to what is being said, and see for yourself the fact that the very first movement of inquiry must be born of freedom. You cannot be committed, and from there inquire, any more than an animal tied to a tree can wander far. Your mind is a slave as long as it is committed to Hinduism, to Buddhism, to Islam, to Christianity, to Communism, or to something it has invented for itself. So we cannot proceed together unless we comprehend from the very beginning, from now on, that to inquire there must be freedom. There must be the abandonment of the past—not unwillingly, grudgingly, but a complete letting go.

After all, the scientists who got together to tackle the problem of going to the moon were free to inquire, however much they may have been slaves to their country, and all the rest of it. I am only referring to that peculiar freedom of the scientist at a research station. At least for the time being, in his laboratory, he is free to inquire. But our laboratory is our living, it is the whole span of life from day to day, from month to month, from year to year, and our freedom to inquire must be total, it cannot be a fragmentary thing, as it is with technical people. That is why, if we are to learn and understand what freedom is, if we are to delve deeply into its unfathomable dimensions, we must from the very start abandon all our commitments, and stand alone. And this is a very difficult thing to do.

The other day in Kashmir, several sannyasis said to me, "We live alone in the snow. We never see anybody. No one ever comes to visit us." And I said to them, "Are you really alone, or are you merely physically separated from humanity?" "Oh, yes," they replied, "we are alone." But they were with their Vedas and Upanishads, with their experiences and gathered knowledge, with their meditations and practices. They were still carrying the burden of their conditioning. That is not being alone. Such men, having put on a saffron cloth, say to themselves, "We have renounced the world." But they have not. You can never renounce the world, because the world is part of you. You may renounce a few cows, a house, some property, but to renounce your heredity, your tradition, your accumulated racial experience, the whole burden of your conditioning—this requires an enormous inquiry, a searching out, which is the movement of learning. The other way—becoming a monk or a hermit—is very easy.

So do consider and see how your job, your going from the house to the office every day for thirty, forty, or fifty years, your knowledge of certain techniques as an engineer, a lawyer, a mathematician, a lecturer—how all this makes you a slave. Of course, in this world one has to know some technique and hold a job, but consider how all these things are narrowing down the margin of freedom. Prosperity, progress, security, success—everything is narrowing down the mind, so that ultimately, or even now, the mind becomes mechanical and carries on by merely repeating certain things it has learned.

A mind that wants to inquire into freedom and discover its beauty, its vastness, its dynamism, its strange quality of not being effective in the worldly sense of that word—such a mind from the very beginning must put aside its commitments, the desire to belong, and with that freedom, it must inquire. Many questions are involved in this. What is the state of the mind that is free to inquire? What does it mean to be free from commitments? Is a married man to free himself from his commitments? Surely, where there is love, there is no commitment; you do not belong to your wife, and your wife does not belong to you. But we do belong to each other, because we have never felt this extraordinary thing called love, and that is our difficulty. We have committed ourselves in marriage, just as we have committed ourselves in learning a technique. Love is not commitment, but again, that is a very difficult thing to understand, because the word is not the thing. To be sensitive to another, to have that pure feeling uncorrupted by the intellect—surely, that is love.

I do not know if you have considered the nature of the intellect. The intellect and its activities are all right at a certain level, are they not? But when the intellect interferes with that pure feeling, then mediocrity sets in. To know the function of the intellect, and to be aware of that pure feeling, without letting the two mingle and destroy each other, requires a very clear, sharp awareness.

Now, when we say that we must inquire into something, is there in fact any inquiring to be done, or is there only direct perception? Do you understand? I hope I am making myself clear. Inquiry is generally a process of analysing and coming to a conclusion. That is the function of the mind, of the intellect, is it not? The intellect says, "I have analysed, and this is the conclusion I have come to." From that conclusion it moves to another conclusion, and so it keeps going.

Surely, when thought springs from a conclusion, it is no longer thinking, because the mind has already concluded. There is thinking only when there is no conclusion. This again you will have to ponder over, neither accepting nor rejecting it. If I conclude that Communism, or Catholicism, or some other "ism" is so, I have stopped thinking. If I conclude that there is god, or that there is no god, I have ceased to inquire. Conclusion takes the form of belief. If I am to find out whether there is god, or what is the true function of the State in relation to the individual, I can never start from a conclusion, because the conclusion is a form of commitment.

So the function of the intellect is always, is it not, to inquire, to analyse, to search out; but because we want to be secure inwardly, psychologically, because we are afraid, anxious about life, we come to some form of conclusion, to which we are committed. From one commitment we proceed to another, and I say that such a mind, such an intellect, being slave to a conclusion, has ceased to think, to inquire.

I do not know if you have observed what an enormous part the intellect plays in our life. The newspapers, the magazines, everything about us is cultivating reason. Not that I am against reason. On the contrary, one must have the capacity to reason very clearly, sharply. But if you observe you find that the intellect is everlastingly analysing why we belong or do not belong, why one must be an outsider to find reality, and so on. We have learned the process of analysing ourselves. So there is the intellect with its capacity to inquire, to analyse, to reason, and come to conclusions, and there is feeling, pure feeling, which is always being interrupted, coloured by the intellect. And when the intellect interferes with pure feeling, out of this interference grows a mediocre mind. On the one hand we have intellect, with its capacity to reason based upon its likes and dislikes, upon its conditioning, upon its experience and knowledge, and on the other, we have feeling, which is corrupted by society, by fear. And will these two reveal what is true? Or is there only perception, and nothing else? I am afraid I am not making myself clear. I will explain what I mean.

To me there is only perception—which is to see something as false or true immediately. This immediate perception of what is false and what is true is the essential factor—not the intellect, with its reasoning based upon its cunning, its knowledge, its commitments. It must sometimes have happened to you that you have seen the truth of something immediately—such as the truth that you cannot belong to anything. That is perception: seeing the truth of something immediately, without analysis, without reasoning, without all the things that the intellect creates in order to postpone perception. It is entirely different from "intuition," which is a word that we use with glibness and ease. And perception has nothing to do with experience. Experience tells you that you must belong to something, otherwise you will be destroyed, you will lose your job, or your family, or your property, or your position and prestige.

So the intellect, with all its reasoning, with its cunning evaluations, with its conditioned thinking, says that you must belong to something, that you must commit yourself in order to survive. But if you perceive the truth that the individual must stand completely alone, then that very perception is a liberating factor; you do not have to struggle to be alone.

To me there is only this direct perception—not reasoning, not calculation, not analysis. You must have the capacity to analyse; you must have a good, sharp mind in order to reason, but a mind that is limited to reason and analysis is incapable of perceiving what is truth. To perceive immediately the truth that it is folly to belong to any religious organization, you must be able to look into your heart of hearts, to know it thoroughly, without all the obstructions created by the intellect. If you commune with yourself, you will know why you belong, why you have committed yourself, and if you push further, you will see the slavery, the cutting down of freedom, the lack of human dignity that commitment entails. When you perceive all this instantaneously, you are free; you don't have to make an effort to be free. That is why perception is essential. All efforts to be free come from self-contradiction. We make an effort because we are in a state of contradiction within ourselves, and this contradiction, this effort, breeds many avenues of escape that hold us everlastingly in the treadmill of slavery.

So it seems to me that one must be very serious—but I do not mean serious in the sense of being committed to something. People who are committed to something are not serious at all. They have given themselves over to something in order to achieve their own ends, in order to enhance their own position or prestige. Such people I do not call serious. The serious man is he who wants to find out what is freedom, and for this he must surely inquire into his own slavery. Don't say you are not a slave. You belong to something, and that is slavery, though your leaders talk of freedom. So did Hitler; so did Khrushchev. Every tyrant, every guru, every president or vice-president, everyone in the whole religious and political set-up, talks of freedom. But freedom is something entirely different. It is a precious fruit without which you lose human dignity. It is love, without which you will never find god, or truth, or that nameless thing. Do what you will—cultivate all the virtues, sacrifice, slave, search out ways to serve man—without freedom, none of these will bring to light that reality within your own heart. That reality, that immeasurable something, comes when there is freedom—the total inward freedom that exists only when you have not committed yourself, when you do not belong to anything, when you are able to stand completely alone without bitterness, without cynicism, without hope or disappointment. Only such a mind-heart is capable of receiving that which is immeasurable.

Bombay, 23 December 1959

To go into ourselves deeply, fully, a sense of freedom is necessary—not at the end, but at the very beginning. Do not ask how to arrive at that freedom. No system of meditation, no book, no drug, no psychological trick you can play on yourself, will give you freedom. Freedom is born of the perception that freedom is essential. The moment you perceive that freedom is essential, you are in a state of revolt—revolt against this ugly world, against all orthodoxy, against tradition, against leadership, both political and religious. Revolt within the framework of the mind soon withers away, but there is a lasting revolt that comes into being when you perceive for yourself that freedom is essential.

Unfortunately, most of us are not aware of ourselves. We have never given thought to the ways of our minds as we have given thought to our techniques, to our jobs. We have never really looked at ourselves; we have never wandered into the depths of ourselves without calculation, without premeditation, without seeking something out of those depths. We have never taken the journey into ourselves without a purpose. The moment one has a motive, a purpose, one is a slave to it; one cannot wander freely within oneself, because one is always thinking in terms of change, of self-improvement. One is tied to the post of self-improvement, which is a projection of one's own narrow, petty mind.

Do please consider what I am saying, not merely verbally, but observe your own mind, the actuality of your inner state. As long as you are a slave, your muttering about god, about truth, about all the things that you have learned from sacred books, has no meaning; it only perpetuates your slavery. But if your mind begins to perceive the necessity of freedom, it will create its own energy, which will then operate without your calculated efforts to be free of slavery.

So we are concerned with the freedom of the individual. But to discover the individual is very difficult, because at present we are not individuals. We are the product of our environment, of our culture; we are the product of the food we eat, of our climate, our customs, our traditions. Surely that is not individuality. I think individuality comes into being only when one is fully aware of this encroaching movement of environment and tradition that makes the mind a slave. As long as I accept the dictates of tradition, of a particular culture, as long as I carry the weight of my memories, my experiences—which after all are the result of my conditioning—I am not an individual but merely a product.

Varanasi, 24 January 1960

ONE CAN SEE, through reading the newspapers and being observant of the events that are going on in the world, that freedom is
getting less and less; the margin of freedom is narrowing down. Do
you know what I mean? The mind has very little chance to be free,
it is not able to think out, to feel out, to discover, because organized religions throughout the world, with their dogmatic beliefs,
have crippled our thinking; superstitions and traditions have
enclosed the mind, conditioned the mind. You are a Hindu, a
Christian, a Moslem, or you belong to some other organized belief
that has been imposed upon you from childhood, and you function
within that circle of limitation, narrow or wide. When you say you
are a Hindu, a Moslem, or what you will, please observe your own
mind. Are you not merely repeating what you have been told? You
do not know, you merely accept—and you accept because it is convenient. Socially, economically it gives you security to accept and
live within that circle. So freedom is denied—not only to the
Hindu, to the Christian, to the Moslem—but to all who are held
within the enclosure of an organized religion.

And if you observe you will see that whatever profession
you belong to is also enslaving you. How can a man be free who
has spent forty years in a particular profession? Look what happens
to a doctor. Having spent seven years or so in college, for the rest of
his life he is a general practitioner or a specialist, and he becomes

enslaved by the profession. Surely his margin of freedom is very narrow. And the same is true of the politicians, of the social reformers, of the people who have ideals, who have an objective in life.

So if you are observant you will see that everywhere in the world the margin of freedom and human dignity is getting less and less. Our minds are mere machines. We learn a profession and forever after we are its slaves. And it seems to me that it requires a great deal of understanding, real perception, insight, to break this circle that the mind and society have woven around each one of us. To approach these enslavements anew, to tackle them fundamentally, deeply, radically, I think one has to be revolutionary—which means thinking, feeling totally, and not just looking at things from the outside. And one must have a sense of humility, must one not?

I do not think humility is a cultivated virtue. Cultivated virtue is a horror, because the moment you cultivate a virtue, it ceases to be a virtue. Virtue is spontaneous, timeless, it is ever active in the present. A mind that merely cultivates humility can never know the fullness, the depth, the beauty of being really humble, and if the mind is not in that state, I do not think it can learn. It can function mechanically, but learning, surely, is not the mechanical accumulation of knowledge. The movement of learning is something entirely different. And to learn, the mind must have a sense of great humility.

I want to know what freedom is—not speculative freedom, which is self-projected as a reaction to something. Is there such a thing as real freedom—a state in which the mind is actually freeing itself from all the traditions and patterns that have been imposed upon it for centuries? I want to know what is this extraordinary thing after which people have struggled through the ages; I want to find out, learn all about it. And how can I do that if I have no sense of humility? Humility has nothing whatsoever to do with the self-protective humbleness that the mind imposes upon itself. That is an ugly thing. Humility cannot be cultivated, and it is surely one of the most difficult things to experience because we have already established ourselves in certain positions. We have certain ideas, values, we have a certain amount of experience, knowledge, and this background dictates our activities, our thoughts. An old man who has accumulated knowledge through his own experiences and through the experiences of others, and who is driven by his urge to be important, to establish for himself a position of power, prestige— how can such a man be in a state of humility and thereby learn about his own trivialities? So it seems to me that we have to be tremendously attentive and deeply aware of this sense of humility.

Ojai, 21 May 1960

HOWEVER MUCH PROGRESS we may make in this world, however far we may go into the skies, visit the moon, Venus, and all the rest of it, the lives of most of us are still very shallow, superficial; they are still outward. And it is much more difficult to go inward; there is no technique for it, no professor to teach it, no laboratory where you can learn to travel within. There is no teacher who can guide you and—please believe me—there is no authority of any kind that can help you to investigate this complex entity called the mind. You have to do it entirely by yourself, without depending on a thing. And as modern civilization is becoming more and more complex, more and more outward, progressive, there is a tendency for all of us to live still more superficially, is there not? We attend more concerts, we read more clever books, we go endlessly to the cinema, we gather together to discuss intellectually, we investigate ourselves psychologically with the help of analysts, and so on. Or, because we live such superficial lives, we turn to churches and fill our minds with their dogmas, both unreasonable and reasonable, with beliefs that are almost absurd, or we escape into some form of mysticism. In other words, realizing that our everyday living is shallow, most of us try to run away from it. We engage our minds in speculative philosophies, or in what we call meditation, contemplation, which is a form of self-hypnosis, or if we are at all intellectual, we create a thought-world of our own in which we live satisfied, intellectually content.

Seeing this whole process, it seems to me that the problem is not what to do, or how to live, or what the immediate action to be taken is when we are confronted with war, with the catastrophes that are actually going on in the world, but, rather, how to inquire into freedom. Because without freedom, there is no creation. By freedom I do not mean the freedom to do what you like: to get into a car and zip along a road, or to think what you like, or to engage yourself in some particular activity. It seems to me that such forms of freedom are not really freedom at all. But is there a freedom of the mind? As most of us do not live in a creative state, I think it is imperative for any thoughtful serious man to inquire very profoundly and very earnestly into this question.

If you observe, you will see that the margin of freedom is getting very, very narrow; politically, religiously, technologically, our minds are being shaped, and our everyday life is diminishing that quality of freedom. The more civilized we become, the less there is of freedom. I do not know if you have noticed how civilization is making us into technicians, and a mind that is built around a technique is not a free mind. A mind that is shaped by a church, by dogmas, by organized religion, is not a free mind. A mind that is darkened by knowledge is not a free mind. If we observe ourselves, it soon becomes obvious that our minds are weighed down by knowledge—we know so much. Our minds are bound by the beliefs and dogmas that organized religions throughout the world have laid upon them. Our education is largely a process of acquiring more technique in order to earn a better livelihood, and everything about us is shaping our minds, every form of influence is directing, controlling us. So the margin of freedom is getting narrower and narrower. The terrible weight of respectability, the acceptance of public opinion, our own fears, anxieties—all these things, surely, if one is at all aware of them, are diminishing the quality of freedom. And this is what, perhaps, we can discuss and understand: how can one free the mind, and yet live in this world with all its techniques, knowledge, experiences? I think this is the problem, the central issue, not only in this country, but in India, in Europe, and all over the world. We are not creative, we are becoming mechanical. I do not mean by creativeness merely writing a poem, or painting a picture, or inventing a new thing. Those are merely the capacities of a talented mind. I mean a state that is creation itself.

But we shall go into all that when we understand the central issue: that our minds are becoming more and more conditioned, that the margin of freedom is getting less and less. We are either Americans, with all the emotional, nationalistic quality behind the flag, or we are Russians, Indians, this or that. We are separated by frontiers, by dogmas, by conflicting ways of thinking, by different categories of organized religious thought; we are separated politically, religiously, economically, and culturally. And if you examine this whole process that is taking place around us, you will see that as individual human beings we count for very little; we are almost nothing at all.

We have many problems, individually as well as collectively. Individually, perhaps, we shall be able to solve some of them, and collectively we shall do what we can. But all these problems, surely, are not the main issue. It seems to me that the main issue is to free the mind, and one cannot free the mind, or the mind cannot free itself, until it understands itself. Therefore self-knowledge is essential: the knowing of oneself. That requires a certain quality of awareness; because, if one doesn't know oneself, there is no basis for reasoning, for thought. But knowing and knowledge are two different things. Knowing is a constant process, whereas knowledge is always static.

I do not know if that point is clear; if not, perhaps I can make it clear as we go along. But what I want to do now is merely to point out certain things, and later on we can investigate them. We have to begin by seeing the overall picture—not concentrating on any particular point, on any particular problem or action, but looking at the whole of our existence, as it were. Once having seen this extraordinary picture of ourselves as we are, we can then take the book of ourselves and go into it chapter by chapter, page by page.

So to me the central problem is freedom. Freedom is not from something; that is only a reaction. Freedom, I feel, is something entirely different. If I'm free from fear, that is one thing. The freedom from fear is a reaction, which only brings about a certain courage. But I'm talking of freedom which is not from something, which is not a reaction; and that requires a great deal of understanding.

I would like to suggest that those who listen should give some time to thinking over what we have been discussing. We are not refusing or accepting anything, because I am not in any way your authority; I am not setting myself up as a teacher. To me, there is no teacher, there is no follower—and please believe me, I mean this very earnestly. I am not your teacher, so you are not my followers. The moment you follow, you are bound, you are not free. If you accept any theory, you are bound by that theory; if you practise any system, however complicated, however ancient or modern it may be, you are a slave to that system.

What we are trying to do is to investigate, to find out together. You are not merely listening to what I point out, but in listening you are trying to discover for yourself, so that you are free. The person who is speaking is of no value, but what is said, what is uncovered, what one discovers for oneself, is of the highest importance. All this personality cult, this personal following, or the putting up of a person in authority, is utterly detrimental. What is of importance is what you discover in your investigation of how to free the mind, so that as a human being you are creative.

After all, reality, or that which is not expressible in words, cannot be found by a mind that is clogged, weighed down. There is, I think, a state, call it what you will, which is not the experience of any saint, of any seeker, of any person who is endeavouring to find it, because all experience is really a perpetuation of the past. Experience only strengthens the past; therefore experience does not free the mind. The freeing element is the state of the mind that is capable of experiencing without the entity who experiences. This again requires a certain explanation, and we shall go into it.

What I do want to say now is that there is a great deal of disturbance, a great deal of uncertainty, not only individually, but also in the world, and because of this disturbance, this uncertainty, there has arisen every kind of philosophy: the philosophy of despair, the philosophy of living in the immediate, of accepting existence as it is. There is a breaking away from traditions, from acceptance, and the building of a world of reaction. Or, leaving one religion, you go to another; if you are a Catholic, you drop Catholicism and become a Hindu, or join some other group. Surely none of these responses will in any way help the mind to be free.

To bring about this freedom, there must be self-knowledge: knowing the way you think and discovering in that process the whole structure of the mind. You know, fact is one thing, and symbol is another; the word is one thing, and what the word represents is another. For most of us, the symbol—the symbol of the flag, the symbol of the cross—has become extraordinarily important, so we live by symbols, by words. But the word, the symbol, is never important. And to break down the word, the symbol, to go behind it, is an astonishingly difficult task. To free the mind from the words—"you are an American, you are a Catholic, you are a democrat, or a Russian, or a Hindu"—is very arduous. And yet if we would inquire into what is freedom, we must break down the symbol, the word. The frontier of the mind is laid down by our education, by the acceptance of the culture in which we have been brought up, by the technology that is part of our heritage, and to penetrate all these layers that condition our thinking requires a very alert, intense mind.

I think it is most important from the very beginning to understand that these talks are not meant in any way to direct or control your thinking or to shape your mind. Our problem is much too great to be solved by belonging to some organization, or by hearing some speaker, by accepting a philosophy from the Orient, or getting lost in Zen Buddhism, by finding a new technique of meditation, or by having new visions through the use of mescaline or some other drug. What we need is a very clear mind—a mind that is not afraid to investigate, a mind that is capable of being alone, that can face its own loneliness, its own emptiness, a mind that is capable of destroying itself to find out.

So I would point out to all of you the importance of being really serious; you are not coming to this for entertainment, or out of curiosity. All that is a waste of time. There is something much deeper, wider, which we have to discover for ourselves: how to go beyond the limitations of our own consciousness. Because all consciousness is a limitation, and all change within consciousness is no change at all. And I think it is possible—not mystically, not in a state of illusion, but actually—to go beyond the frontiers that the mind has laid down. But one can do that only when one is capable of investigating the quality of the mind and having really profound knowledge of oneself. Without knowing yourself, you cannot go far, because you will get lost in an illusion, you will escape into fanciful ideas, into some new form of sectarianism.

❖

SO CONSIDERING ALL these many aspects of our living, our main problem, as the speaker sees it, is this question of freedom. Because it is only in freedom that we can discover; it is only in freedom that there can be the creative mind; it is only when the mind is free that there is endless energy—and it is this energy that is the movement of reality.

To conclude I would suggest that you consider, observe, and be aware of the enslavement of your own mind. What has been said so far is merely an outline of the contents of the book, and if you are content with the outline, with the headlines, with a few ideas, then I'm afraid you will not go very far. It is not a matter of acceptance or denial, but rather of inquiry into yourself—which does not demand any form of authority. On the contrary, it demands that you should follow nobody, that you should be a light unto yourself, and you cannot be a light unto yourself if you are committed to any particular mode of conduct, to any form of activity that has been laid down as being respectable, as being religious. One must begin very near to go very far, and one cannot go very far if one does not know oneself. The knowing of oneself does not depend on any analyst. One can observe oneself as one goes along in every form of relationship, every day, and without that understanding, the mind can never be free.

Varanasi, 1 January 1962

I THINK MOST of us regard individual action as unimportant while there is so much collective action necessary. For most of us, individual action is generally opposed to collective action. Most of us consider that collective action is much more important and has greater significance for society than individual action. For us individual action leads nowhere, it is not sufficiently significant or creative enough, to bring about a definite change of order, a definite revolution in society. So we regard collective action as much more impressive, much more urgent than individual action. Particularly in a world that is becoming more and more technically minded and mechanically minded, individual action has very little place, and so gradually the importance of the individual diminishes and the collective becomes all important.

One can observe this taking place when the mind of man is being taken over, is being collectivized—if I may use that word—is being forced to conform much more than ever before. The mind is no longer free. It is being shaped by politics, by education, by religious organized belief and dogma. Everywhere throughout the world, freedom is becoming less and less, and the individual is becoming less and less significant. You must have observed this, not only in your lives but also generally, that freedom has withered away—freedom to think quite independently, freedom to stand up for something that you think is right, freedom to say "no" to established order, freedom to discover, to question, to find out for yourself. More and more, leadership is becoming important, because we want to be told, we want to be guided. And unfortunately, when this takes place, corruption is inevitable, there is deterioration of the mind—not the technical mind, not the capacity to build bridges, atomic reactors, and so on—but deterioration of the quality of the mind that is creative. I am using that word *creative* in quite a different way from the usual one. I do not mean creative in the sense of writing a poem or building a bridge or putting down, in marble or in stone, a vision that is being caught— those are mere expressions of what one feels or what one thinks. But we are talking of a creative mind in quite a different sense: a mind that is free, is creative; a mind that is not bound by dogmas, by beliefs; a mind that has not taken shelter within the limits of experience; a mind that breaks through the barriers of tradition, of authority, of ambition; that is no longer within the net of envy— such a mind is a creative mind. And it seems to me that in a world where there is the threat of war, where there is general deterioration, not technologically but in every other way, such a creative, free mind is necessary.

It is absolutely, urgently necessary to alter the whole course of human thought, of human existence, because it is becoming more and more mechanistic. And I do not see how this complete revolution can take place except in the individual. The collective cannot be revolutionary; the collective can only follow, can only adjust itself, can imitate, can conform. But it is only the individual, the "you," that can break through, shattering all these conditionings, and be creative. It is the crisis in consciousness that demands this mind, this new mind. And apparently, from what one observes, one never thinks along these lines, but one is always thinking that more improvement—technological, mechanistic improvement—will bring about in some miraculous way the creative mind, the mind that is free from fear.

So we are going to concern ourselves not with the improvement of the technical processes that are necessary in the collective world of mechanistic action but rather how to bring about this creative mind, this new mind. Because in this country, as one sees, there is a general decline, except perhaps industrially, in making more money, in building railways, dredging canals, dredging rivers, iron works, manufacturing more goods—which are all necessary. But that is not going to bring about a new civilization. That will bring progress, but progress, as one observes, does not bring freedom to man. Things are necessary, goods are necessary; more shelter, more clothes, and more food are absolutely necessary; but there is the other thing that is also equally necessary—the individual who says "no."

To say "no" is much more important than to say "yes." We all say "yes" and we never say "no" and stand by "no." It is very difficult to deny, and very easy to conform, and most of us do conform because it is so easy to slip into conformity through fear, through desire for security, and thereby gradually to stagnate, disintegrate. But to say "no" requires the highest form of thinking, because to say "no" implies negative thinking—that is to see what is false. The very perception of what is false, the clarity with which one sees what is false, that very perception is creative action. The denial of something, the questioning of something—however sacred, however powerful, however well established—requires deep penetration, requires the shattering of one's own ideas, traditions. And such an individual is absolutely essential in the modern world where propaganda, where organized religion, the make-believe is taking over. I do not know if you also see the importance of this—not verbally, not theoretically, but actually.

You know there is a way of looking at things. Either we look at them directly, experience the thing that we see, or we examine what we see, verbally, intellectually, we spin theories about "what is" and find explanations for "what is." But without finding explanations, without mere judgment, which we will also come to later, to perceive directly something as false requires attention, requires all your capacity. And apparently, especially in this unfortunate country where tradition, authority, and the ancient so-called wisdom rule and dominate, that energetic quality to see what is false, to deny it and to stand by that denial seems to be utterly lacking. But to inquire into what is false requires a free mind. You cannot ask if you have committed yourself to a particular form of belief, to a particular form of experience, to a certain course of action. If you have committed yourself to a particular pattern of government, you cannot question, you dare not question, because you lose your position, your influence, the things that you are afraid of losing. And also when you are committed to a particular form of religion as a Hindu, a Buddhist, or what not, you dare not question, you dare not tear through, destroy everything to find out. But unfortunately most of us are committed politically, economically, socially, or religiously, and from there, from that commitment, we never question the very centre, the very thing to which we are committed. Therefore, we are always seeking freedom in ideas, in books, in a lot of words.

So I would suggest, if I may, that while you listen, you not only hear the words, which are only a means of communication, a symbol that needs to be interpreted by each one, but also, through the words, that you discover your own state of mind, discover the things to which you are committed yourself, discover for yourself the things to which you are tied hand and foot, mind and heart—actually discover it and see whether it is possible to break down the things to which you are committed, to find out what is true. Because I do not see otherwise how a regeneration is to take place in the world. There will be social upheavals—whether communistic or otherwise; there will be more prosperity, more food, more factories, more fertilizers, more engines and so on. But surely that is not all life, that is only a part of life. And to worship and live in the fragment does not solve our human problems. There is still sorrow, there is still death, there is still anxiety, guilt, the aches of many ideas, hopes, despairs: they are all there.

So in listening, I would suggest that it should be rather the listening of a mind that is self-examining—examining its own processes rather than listening to words with which it agrees or disagrees, which is of very little importance. Because we are dealing only with facts: the fact that human beings are becoming more and more mechanical; the fact that there is less and less freedom; the fact that when there is confusion, authority is resorted to; and the fact that there is conflict outwardly as war and inwardly as misery, despair, fear. These are all facts to deal with, not theoretically but actually. So what we are concerned with is how to bring about a change—a radical revolution in the individual—in the listener, because he is the only one that can be creative, not the politician, not the leader, not the important man; they have committed themselves, and they have settled down in a groove. And they want fame; they want power, position. You also may want them, but you are still feeling your way toward them, so there is still some hope, because you are not completely committed, you are not the big men of the land. You are still small people, you are not leaders, you have no tremendous organizations over which you are the bosses, you are just ordinary average men. And being fairly uncommitted, you have still some hope.

Therefore, it may be possible, though at the eleventh hour, to bring about this change in ourselves. And so that is the only thing with which we are concerned: how to bring about this tremendous revolution within ourselves.

Most of us change through compulsion, through some outside influence, through fear, through punishment, or through reward—that is the only thing that will make us change. Do follow this, sirs, observe all this. We never change voluntarily, we always change with a motive, and a change through a motive is no change at all. And to be aware of the motives, of the influences, of the compulsions that force us to change, to be aware of them and to deny them is to bring about change. Circumstances make us change; the family, the law, our ambitions, our fears bring about a change. But that change is a reaction and therefore really it is a resistance, a psychological resistance to a compulsion. That resistance creates its own modification, change, and therefore it is no change at all. If I change or if I adjust myself to society because I expect something from society, is that a change? Or does mutation take place only when I see the things that are compelling me to change, and see their falseness? All influences, whether good or bad, condition the mind, and merely to accept such conditioning is inwardly to resist any form of change, any radical change.

So, seeing the situation, not only in this country but throughout the world, where progress is denying freedom, where prosperity is making the mind more and more secure in things and therefore there is less and less freedom, where religious organizations are taking over more and more the formula of belief that will make man believe in god or in no god, seeing that the mind is becoming more and more mechanistic, and also observing that the electronic brains and the modern technological knowledge are giving man more and more leisure—not yet everywhere, but it will come—seeing all this, we have to find out what is freedom, what is reality.

These questions cannot be answered by a mechanical mind. One has to put the questions to oneself fundamentally, deeply, inwardly, and find the answers for oneself, if there are answers—which means really questioning all authority. Apparently, that is one of the most difficult things to do. We never regard society as the enemy. We regard society as something with which we have to live; we conform and adjust ourselves to it; we never think it is really the enemy of man, the enemy of freedom, the enemy of righteousness. Do think about it; look at it. Environment, which is society, is destroying freedom. It does not want a man who is free, it wants the saints, the reformers who would modify, bolster, uphold the social institutions. But religion is something entirely different. The religious man is the enemy of society. The religious man is not a man who goes to church or goes to a temple, reads the Gita, does puja every day; *he* is not really religious at all. A really religious man has got rid of all ambition, envy, greed, fear, so that he has a mind that is young, fresh, new, so as to investigate, to find out what is beyond all the things that man has put together and that he calls religion. But all this requires a great deal of self-inquiry, an inquiry into oneself, self-knowing, and without that foundation you cannot go very far.

So a mutation, a complete revolution, not a modified change but a complete mutation in the mind is necessary. How to bring this about is the problem. We see it is necessary. Any man who has thought at all, who has observed the state of the world, who is sensitive to what is going on within himself and outside himself, must demand this mutation. But how is one to bring it about?

Now, first of all, is there a "how"—the "how" being the method, the system, the way, the practice? If there is a way, if there is a method, if there is a system, and if you practice it in order to bring about a mutation, your mind is merely a slave to that system; your mind is shaped by that system, by that method, by that practice, and therefore can never be free. It is like saying, "I will discipline myself in order to be free." Freedom and discipline do not go together, which does not mean that you become undisciplined. The very act of "seeking freedom" brings its own discipline. But the mind that has disciplined itself in a system, in a formula, in a belief, in ideas—such a mind can never be free. So one has to see from the very beginning that the "how," which implies practise, discipline, the following of a formula, prevents mutation from taking place. That is the first thing that one has to see, because practise, method, or system becomes the authority that denies freedom and therefore mutation. One has really to see that fact, see the truth of that. I mean by *seeing*, not seeing intellectually, verbally, but being emotionally in contact with that fact. We are emotionally in contact with the fact when we see a snake; there is no question about it, there is a direct challenge and a direct response. In the same way one has to see that any system, however well thought out—it does not matter by whom—does deeply destroy freedom, stop creation, because system implies gaining, an achievement, arriving somewhere, a reward, and therefore is the very denial of freedom. That is why you will follow somebody, because you pursue the medium through which you gain—the medium being some kind of discipline.

But one must see this fact that the mind must be absolutely free—whether it is possible or not, that is quite a different matter—that there must be freedom: otherwise, you become merely mechanical like any glorified machine. One has to see very clearly that freedom is essential. And it is only when there is freedom that you can discover if there is, or if there is not, god or something immense, beyond the measure of man. Then you will begin to question every system, every authority, every structure of society. And the crisis demands this mind. Surely only such a mind can find out what is true. It is only such a mind that can find out if there is, or if there is not, something beyond time, beyond the things that man has put together in his thought.

All this requires immense energy, and the essence of energy is the denial of conflict. A mind that is lost in conflict has no energy, whether the conflict is within oneself or outside with the world. All this requires immense investigation and understanding. And I hope that we can do this: to be aware of the fact and to pursue the fact to its end and see whether the mind, our mind, your mind, can be really free.

New Delhi, 14 February 1962

WE MUST HAVE freedom, not verbal freedom, not mere political freedom nor freedom from organized religions. I think that most people who are aware of the world-situation have gone away from these institutionalized ways of life; though these have had a superficial effect on our lives, deeply they have not had much effect. If one has to find out what is freedom, one must question everything, question every institution—the family, religion, marriage, tradition, the values that society has imposed upon us, education, the whole structure of social and moral organization. But *we* question not to discover what is true, but to find a way out, and therefore we are never psychologically free. We are concerned more with resistance, and not with freedom. I think it is important to understand this.

Saanen, 31 July 1962

WE WERE TALKING the other day about action without idea, because, as I was pointing out, thought is a response of our memory; thought is always limited, conditioned by the past, and it can therefore never bring about freedom.

I think it is very important to understand this fact. Psychologically there can be no freedom at all if the defensive process of thought is not completely understood. And freedom—which is not a reaction to or the opposite of non-freedom—is essential, because it is only in freedom that one can discover. It is only when the mind is totally free that there can be the perception of what is true.

Truth is not something that has continuity and that can be maintained through practice or discipline, but it is something to be seen in a flash. This perception of truth does not come about through any form of conditioned thinking, and therefore it is not possible for thought to imagine, conceive, or formulate what is true.

To understand totally what is true, there must be freedom. For most of us, freedom is only a word, or a reaction, or an intellectual idea that serves as an escape from our bondage, from our sorrow, from our boring daily routine, but that is not freedom at all. Freedom does not come by seeking it; because you cannot seek freedom, it is not to be found. Freedom comes only when we understand the whole process of the mind that creates its own barriers, its own limitations, its own projections from a conditioned and conditioning background.

It is very important for a really religious mind to understand that which is beyond the word, beyond thought, beyond all experience. And to understand that, to be with that which is beyond all experience, to see it in great depth in a flash, the mind must be free. Idea, concept, pattern, opinion, judgment, or any formulated discipline, prevent freedom of the mind. And this freedom brings its own discipline—not the discipline of conformity, of suppression or adjustment, but a discipline that is not the outcome of thought, of motive.

Surely in a confused world where there is so much conflict and misery it is extraordinarily urgent to understand that freedom is the primary requisite of the human mind—not comfort, not a fleeting moment of pleasure or the continuity of that pleasure, but a total freedom, from which alone there can be happiness. For happiness is not an end in itself; like virtue, it is a by-product of freedom. A person who is free is virtuous, but a man who is merely practising virtue by conforming to the pattern established by society can never know what freedom is, and therefore can never be virtuous.

I would like to talk about the quality of freedom and see if we can together feel our way into it, but I do not know how you listen to what is being said. Do you listen merely to the words? Do you listen in order to understand, in order to experience? If you listen in either of these ways, then what is being said will have very little significance. What is important is to listen, not just to the words, or in the hope of experiencing this extraordinary quality of freedom, but to listen without effort, without striving, with a sense of ease. But this demands a certain quality of attention. By attention I mean being completely there with all your mind and heart. And then you will discover for yourself, if you so listen, that this freedom is not a thing to be pursued; it is not the result of thought or of emotional, hysterical demands. Freedom comes without your seeking it when there is total attention. Total attention is the quality of a mind that has no border, no frontier, and is therefore capable of receiving every single impression, seeing and hearing everything. And this can be done, it is not something enormously difficult. It is difficult only because we are so caught up in habits, and that is one of the things I would like to talk about.

❖

WE THINK THAT we can get rid of envy gradually and we make an effort to put it away little by little, thereby introducing the idea of time. We say, "I will try to get rid of envy tomorrow, or a little later on," and in the meantime we are envious. The words *try* and *in the meantime* are the very essence of time, and when you introduce the time factor there can be no freedom from habit. Either you break a habit immediately, or it goes on, gradually dulling the mind and creating further habits.

Now is it possible for the mind to get rid instantly of this idea of gradually arriving somewhere, gradually transcending something, gradually being free? To me, freedom is not a question of time—there is no tomorrow in which to get rid of envy or to acquire some virtue. And if there is no tomorrow, there is no fear. There is only a complete living in the now; all time has ceased and therefore there is no formation of habit. I mean by that word *now* the immediate, and this state of immediacy is not a reaction to the past nor an avoidance of the future. There is only the moment of total awareness; all one's attention is here in the now. Surely, all existence is in the now; whether you have immense gladness, or great sorrow, or whatever it is, it happens only in the immediate. But through memory the mind gathers experience from the past and projects it into the future.

Without freedom from the past there is no freedom at all, because the mind is never new, fresh, innocent. It is only the fresh, innocent mind that is free. Freedom has nothing to do with age, it has nothing to do with experience, and it seems to me that the very essence of freedom lies in understanding the whole mechanism of habit, both conscious and unconscious. It is not a question of ending habit, but of seeing totally the structure of habit. You have to observe how habits are formed and how, by denying or resisting one habit, another habit is created. What matters is to be totally conscious of habit; for then, as you will see for yourself, there is no longer the formation of habit. To resist habit, to fight it, to deny it, only gives continuity to habit. When you fight a particular habit you give life to that habit, and then the very fighting of it becomes a further habit. But if you are simply aware of the whole structure of habit without resistance, then you will find there is freedom from habit, and in that freedom a new thing takes place.

Saanen, 11 July 1963

THOUGH WE TALK of freedom, most of us do not want to be free at all. I do not know if you have observed this fact. In the modern world—where society is so highly organized, where there is more and more "progress," where the production of things is so vast and so easy—one becomes a slave to possessions, to things, and in them one finds security. And security is all that most of us want—physical and emotional security—therefore we really do not want to be free. By freedom I mean total freedom, not freedom along one particular line, and I think we ought to demand it of ourselves, insist upon it.

Freedom is different from revolt. Revolt is against something: you revolt against something and are for something. Revolt is a reaction, but freedom is not. In the state of freedom, you are not free from something. The moment you are free from something, you are really in revolt against that something; therefore you are not free. Freedom is not "from something," but in itself the mind is free. That is an extraordinary feeling—for the mind to be free in itself, to know freedom for its own sake.

Now, unless one is free I do not see how one can be creative. I am not using that word *creative* in the narrow sense of a man who paints a picture, writes a poem, or invents a machine. To me, such people are not creative at all. They may be inspired for the time being, but creation is entirely different. Creation can be only when there is total freedom. In that state of freedom there is a fullness, and then writing a poem, painting a picture, or carving a stone, has a different meaning altogether. It is then not mere self-expression, it is not the result of frustration, it is no longer seeking a market: it is something entirely different. It seems to me that we should demand to know this complete freedom, not only in ourselves but outwardly.

So first I think we should differentiate between freedom on the one hand and revolt or revolution on the other. Revolt and revolution are essentially a reaction. There is the revolt of the extreme left against capitalism, and the revolt against the dominance of the church. There is also the revolt against the police state, against the power of organized tyranny, but nowadays that doesn't pay, because they very quietly liquidate you, put you away.

To me, freedom is something entirely different. Freedom is not a reaction, but rather the state of mind that comes into being when we understand reaction. Reaction is the response to challenge; it is pleasure, anger, fear, psychological pain, and in understanding this very complex structure of response, we shall come upon freedom. Then you will find that freedom is not freedom from anger, from authority, and so on. It is a state *per se*, to be experienced for itself, and not because you are against something.

Most of us are concerned with our own security. We want a companion and hope to find happiness in a particular relationship; we want to be famous, to create, to express, expand, fulfil ourselves; we want to have power, position, prestige. In one degree or another, that is really what most of us are concerned with, and freedom, god, truth, love, become something to be looked for after that. So, as I said, our religion is a superficial thing, a kind of hobby that does not play a very important part in our lives. We are satisfied with trivialities, and therefore there is not the alertness, the perception that is required to understand this complex process, which we call living. Our existence is a constant struggle, a fatuous, endless effort—and for what? It is a cage in which we are caught, a cage that we have built out of our own reactions, out of our fears, despairs, anxieties. All our thinking is a reaction. We went into this the other day when the question was asked: "What is the right function of thought?" We went into it very carefully, and we discovered that all our thinking is a reaction, the response of memory. The whole structure of our consciousness, of our thought, is the residue, the reservoir of our reactions. Obviously, thought can never bring about freedom, because freedom is not the result of a reaction. Freedom is not the rejection of the things that give us pain, nor is it detachment from the things that give us pleasure and to which we have become slaves.

NOW, THE ONLY real freedom is freedom from the known. Please follow this a little bit. It is freedom from the past. The known has its place, obviously. I must know certain things in order to function in everyday life. If I did not know where I lived, I would be lost. And there is the accumulated knowledge of science, of medicine, and the many technologies, to which more and more is being added. All of that is within the field of the known, and it has its place. But the known is always mechanical. Every experience that you have had, whether in the distant past or only yesterday, is within the field of the known, and from that background you recognize all further experience. In the field of the known there is attachment, with its fears, its despairs, and the mind that is held within this field, however extensive, however wide, is not free. It may write very clever books, it may know how to go to the moon, it may invent the most complicated and extraordinary machines—if you have seen some of them you will know how really extraordinary they are—but it is still held within the field of the known.

NOW, FREEDOM FROM all that is freedom from the known; it is the state of a mind that says, "I do not know," and that is not looking for an answer. Such a mind is completely not seeking, not expecting, and it is only in this state that you can say, "I understand." It is the only state in which the mind is free, and from that state you can look at the things that are known—but not the other way round. From the known you cannot possibly see the unknown, but when once you have understood the state of a mind that is free—which is the mind that says, "I don't know" and remains unknowing, and is therefore innocent—from that state you can function, you can be a citizen, you can be married, or what you will. Then what you do has relevance, significance in life. But we remain in the field of the known, with all its conflicts, striving, disputes, agonies, and from that field we try to find that which is unknown; therefore we are not really seeking freedom. What we want is the continuation, the extension of the same old thing: the known.

IF YOU ARE HEARING for the first time this statement that you must be free of thought, you may say, "Poor chap, he is crazy." But if you have really listened, not only this time but for the many years during which some of you have perhaps read all about it, you will know that what is being said has an extraordinary vitality, a penetrating truth. Only the mind that has emptied itself of the known is creative. That is creation. What it creates has nothing to do with it. Freedom from the known is the state of a mind that is in creation. How can a mind that is in creation be concerned with itself? Therefore, to understand that state of mind, you have to know yourself, you have to observe the process of your own thinking—observe it, not to alter, not to change it, but just observe it as you see yourself in a mirror. When there is freedom, then you can use knowledge and it will not destroy humanity. But when there is no freedom and you make use of knowledge, you create misery for everybody, whether you are in Russia, in America, in China, or anywhere else. I call that mind serious that is aware of the conflict of the known and is not caught in it, not trying to modify, to improve the known; for on that path there is no end to sorrow and misery.

Madras, 15 January 1964

Freedom—TO BE FREE—is becoming more and more difficult. As society becomes more complex and as industrialization becomes wider and deeper and more organized, there is less and less freedom for man. As one observes, when the State becomes all-powerful, when there is social welfare, the care of the welfare state over the citizens is so complete that there is less and less freedom, outwardly. And outwardly one becomes a slave to society, to the pressure of society; in this pressure of organized existence there is no longer tribal existence, but industrialized, organized, centralized control. Outwardly, there is less and less freedom. Where there is more "progress," there is less freedom. This is obvious, as you see in every society becoming more complex, more organized.

So outwardly there is the pressure of the control, the shaping of the mind of the individual—technologically, industrially. Being so outwardly held, there is naturally the tendency to become inwardly, psychologically, more and more entrenched in a particular pattern of existence. Again this is an obvious fact. So for one who is serious enough to find out whether there is such a thing as reality, to find out what is truth—the truth not put together by man in his fear, in his despair; the truth that is not a tradition, a repetition, a thing that is an instrument of propaganda—to find that out, there must be complete freedom. Outwardly, perhaps, there may not be freedom; but inwardly, there must be absolute freedom.

And to understand this question of freedom is one of the most difficult things. I do not know if you have gone into it at all, or even if you have thought about it. Do you know what it means to be free? By freedom I do not mean the abstract, ideational freedom, liberation—that is too abstract, too far away; it may have no reality at all; it may be the invention of a mind that is in despair, in fear, in agony, and that has constructed verbally a pattern, hoping to achieve a verbal state but not an actuality. We are talking of freedom, not in abstraction but actually; we are talking of the everyday freedom, inwardly, in which, psychologically, there is no bondage to anything. Is that possible? Theoretically and ideationally it may be possible. But we are not concerned with ideas, with theories, with speculative religious hopes: we are concerned with facts.

TRUTH WHICH IS made manifest by another or described by another or told by another—however wise, however intelligent—is not truth. You have to find it; you have to understand it. I withdraw that word *find*—you cannot find truth; you cannot set about deliberately, consciously, to find it. You must come upon truth darkly, unknowingly. But you cannot come upon it if your mind, if your psyche, is not completely and totally free inwardly.

To discover anything, even in the scientific field, the mind must be free. The mind must be untrammelled to see something new. But most of our minds, unfortunately, are not fresh, young, innocent—to see, to observe, to understand. We are full of experiences, not only the experiences that one has gathered recently—I mean by "recently" within the last fifty, sixty, or hundred years—but also the experience of man, ageless. We are cluttered up with all that which is our knowledge, conscious or unconscious; the conscious knowledge is what we have acquired through education in the modern world, at the present time.

❖

SO A MIND that would understand what is true has to comprehend, not ideationally, the whole significance of what freedom is. Freedom is not liberation in some heavenly world, but is the freedom of every day, freedom from jealousy, freedom from attachment, freedom from ambition, freedom from competition—which is "the more," "I must be better," "I am this and I must become that." But when you observe what you are, there is no becoming something other than what you are; then there is an immediate transformation of that which is.

So a mind that will go very far must begin very near. But you cannot go very far if you merely verbalize on something that man has created as truth, as god. You must begin very near and lay the foundation. And even to lay that foundation, there must be freedom. Therefore you lay your foundation on freedom, *in* freedom. Thus, it is no longer a foundation; it is a movement—it is not something static.

It is only when the mind has understood the extraordinary nature of knowledge, freedom, and learning, that conflict ceases; only then does the mind become very clear, precise. It is not caught in opinions, in judgments; it is in a state of attention, and therefore it is in a state of complete energy and learning. It is only when the mind is still that it can learn—not "learn about what?" It is only the still mind that can learn, and what is important is not what it learns about, but the state of learning, the state of silence in which it is learning.

Bombay, 16 February 1964

THE WORD *freedom* is heavily loaded, politically, religiously, social-ly, and in every way. That word is really an extraordinary word with a tremendous significance and depth; we have loaded it, like "love," with all kinds of meaning. There is political freedom, social freedom, freedom of opportunity to work; there is freedom from religious dogmas, beliefs; freedom from immediate responsibilities, problems, anxiety, fears; freedom from so many things the mind wants. And we have built a verbal structure that gives us the appearance of freedom, but we do not know what it means to be really free, to feel it, not to argue about it, not to define it, not to say: "What do you mean by freedom?" We do not know the quality of it, the feel of it, the demand for it—not at any particular level but totally.

Without total freedom, every perception, every objective regard, is twisted. It is only the man who is totally free who can look and understand immediately. Freedom implies really, doesn't it, the total emptying of the mind. Completely to empty the whole content of the mind—that is real freedom. Freedom is not mere revolt from circumstances, which again breeds other circumstances, other environmental influences, which enslave the mind. We are talking about a freedom that comes naturally, easily, unasked for, when the mind is capable of functioning at its highest level.

Most of our brains are lazy. Our brains have thickened,

have been made dull through education, through specialization, through conflict, through every form of psychological inward struggle as well as outward compulsions. Our brains function only when there is an immediate demand, when there is an immediate crisis. But otherwise we live in a state of hypnotic, monotonous life, functioning lazily with our jobs and tasks; so our brains are not sharp, alert, awake, sensitive, functioning at their highest capacity.

If the brain does not function at its highest capacity, it is not capable of being free. Because a dull, shallow, limited, narrow, petty mind merely reacts to its environment, and through that reaction it becomes a slave to that environment. And from this arises the whole problem of extricating oneself from the environment and not being a slave to every form of influence, direction, urge. So what is important is the quality of feeling to be utterly free.

There are two kinds of freedom: one is the freedom from something, which is a reaction; and the other is not a reaction, it is "being free." The freedom from something is a response, depend-
g on our choice, on our character, on our temperament, on various
ms of conditioning. Such as a boy who is in revolt against soci-
—he wants to be free. Or a husband who wants to be free from
ife, or a wife from the husband; or wanting to be free from
, jealousy, envy, despair. Those are all reactions, responses to
circumstances, which prevent you from functioning freely,

We want personal liberty. And that liberty is denied in a
y where the mores, the customs, the habits, the traditions are
ndously important; then there is a revolt. Or there is a revolt
st tyranny. So there are various forms of revolt, responses to
ediate demands. Really that is not freedom at all, because
ry reaction breeds further reactions, which create further envi-
ments through which the mind becomes a slave again, so there
constant repetition of revolt, being caught by circumstances,
olt against those circumstances and so on, endlessly.

We are talking of a freedom that is not a reaction. The
ind that is free is not a slave to anything, to any circumstances, to

any particular routine; though it is specialized to do a certain functional job, it is not a slave to that, it is not held in that groove; though it lives in society, it is not of society. And a mind that is emptying itself of all the accumulations, of everyday reactions, all the time—it is only such a mind that is free.

We live by action. Action is imperative, it is necessary. There is the action born of idea and there is the action born of freedom. We are going to go into something that needs the quickness of your brain, not your agreement or your disagreement. The house is on fire, the world is on fire, burning, destroying itself, and there must be action. And that action does not depend on your ideas about the fire, on the size of the bucket or what you will do. You act to put out that fire. To put out that fire, you cannot have ideas about that fire: who set the house on fire, what is the nature of the fire, so on and on, speculating about the fire. There must be immediate action. This means the mind must undergo a complete mutation.

Man has lived for nearly two million years biologically. H has accumulated so many experiences, so much knowledge, a has lived through so many civilizations, so many pressures strains. You are that man, whether you know it or not. Whethe acknowledge it or not, you are that man, you are the result o million years. Either you continue evolving slowly through suffering, anxiety, all kinds of conflicts, endlessly, or you st of that current altogether, at any time, like stepping off a bo the bank of the river—you can do that at any time. And it the free mind that can do it.

❖

To UNDERSTAND WHAT is freedom and action, you must un stand the whole process of your own thinking; that is, you m know yourself. And that is one of the most difficult tasks that can possibly undertake. Because to know oneself implies a m that is capable of looking at itself without the previous knowled it has acquired. If you look at yourself with the knowledge that y have got, then you are merely projecting or translating what you see according to the past, and therefore not looking at yourself. So to look at yourself demands a freshness of mind each minute. That is where the arduousness comes in. Please understand this. Because if you do not understand what is being said now, then when I go into the problem of freedom, you will not be able to take it up and go into it.

IF WE OBSERVE ourselves, we shall find that most of us respond according to our knowledge, according to our experience, according to our conditioning either as a Hindu, or a Buddhist, or a Christian, or a Communist, or a technician, or a family man. Such a man has acquired lots of experience, and having accumulated, he reacts. And with that knowledge he looks at himself. Then he says: "This is good," "This is bad," "This I must keep," "This I must reject." When he does that, he is not looking at himself; he is merely projecting his knowledge upon what he sees, and translating or interpreting what he sees in terms of his experience, knowledge, and conditioning.

PLEASE WATCH YOURSELF. See how insensitive your mind has become. When you have a feeling of pleasure or pain, of a spontaneous joy of something, the moment you feel it there is an immediate response to it by naming it; you name it instantly. Please follow this, observe it in yourself. Because if you don't follow all this, when I talk about freedom, it will mean nothing to you. I am talking about a mind that does not name. When you have a feeling, you name it instantly, you give it a name. The very process of naming it is the state of non-observation. You name it in order to fix it as an experience in your memory, and then, the next day, that memory, which has become mechanical, wants it repeated. Therefore when you look at the sunset the next day, it is no longer the thing that you looked at spontaneously, the first day. So the naming process of any feeling, in any observation, prevents you from looking.

AND TO KNOW yourself is the most arduous task that you can set yourself. You can go to the moon, you can do everything in life, but if you don't know yourself, you will be empty, dull, stupid. Though you may function as a prime minister or a first class engineer or a marvellous technician, you are merely functioning mechanically. So feel the importance, the seriousness of knowing yourself—not what people have said about you, whether you are the supreme self or the little self. Wipe away all the things that people have said, and observe your own minds and your own hearts, and from there function.

ALL OUR IDEALS, however sublime, however lovely, however beautiful, have no meaning. Because they create conflict between what is and what should be. What is important is what is, and not what should be. Please do understand this very simple psychological fact: what is important is what is. You are angry, you are violent, you are cruel, you are hateful, you dislike, and you protect your security at any cost—these are facts, not your non-violence, *ahimsa*, which is sheer nonsense. When you observe what is, without the ideal—which is a distraction from what is, an avoidance of what is—then you either say, "Well, I accept what is and will live with it, be miserable with it," or you have a direct action upon it, or it has a direct action upon you. So what is important is to be capable of observing actually what is—whether you are angry, lustful, wanting this and that. You know what human beings are inwardly. To observe it without naming it, without saying, "I am angry, I must not be angry," but just to observe it, to know what it means, the depth, the extraordinary feeling that lies behind all the subtleties, the secrets—if you so observe, then you will see that out of that observation there is freedom, and out of that freedom there is action immediately.

The innocent mind has space like a child within the mother's womb. But a mind that is crowded, that is heavy with its own despairs, fears, joys, pleasures—such a mind is never empty, and therefore there is nothing new for it, nothing new can come. It is only in that emptiness that a new thing, a new mutation, can take place. This emptiness, this space, is freedom. And for the space to come about, you have to understand this whole structure of yourself, the conscious as well as the unconscious.

And therefore freedom is not a reaction. Freedom is a state of being. Freedom is a feeling. You have to liberate yourself, free yourself, even in little things: you dominating your wife, or your wife dominating you, or your ambitions, your greeds, your envy. When you cut through all that, not taking time and discussing it, then you will see that, without analysis, without introspective moods and demands, to observe—to see things as they are without self-pity, without the desire to change, just to observe—is to have that space.

And the moment there is that space untouched by society, then in that state there is a mutation, a mutation takes place. And you need a mutation in this world, because that mutation is the birth of the individual. And it is only the individual that can do something in this world, to bring about a complete revolution, a complete change, a complete transformation. What we need in this world at the present time is an individual who is born out of this emptiness.

Bombay, 1 March 1964

Please listen to this. We seek help because we are in a state of misery, confusion, conflict, and we want to be helped. We want somebody to tell us what to do. We want some guidance; we want to take somebody's hand in this darkness who will take us to the light. We are so confused, we do not know where to turn. Education, religion, leaders, saints—all these have utterly failed, and yet, because we are in sorrow, because there is conflict and confusion, we look to somebody to help us. And probably that is why most of you are here, hoping in some way to catch a glimpse of reality, hoping in some way to be led to that beauty of life.

Now, if you will kindly listen with your inner ear, with clarity, you will see that there is no help. The speaker cannot help you; he refuses to help you. Please understand this. Go with it slowly. He refuses totally, completely, to help you.

What you want is to sustain the corruption, live in corruption, and to have help in that corruption. You want to be helped a little bit to live comfortably, to carry on with your ambitions, with your ways, with your envies, with your brutalities; to continue in the everyday existence, and yet modify it a little—become a little more rich, a little more comfortable, a little more happy. That is all you want: a better job, a better car, a better position. You really do not want to be completely, entirely, free of sorrow. You don't want to find out what is love, and the beauty of it, the immensity of it. You don't want to find out what is creation.

What you really want is to be helped to continue in a modified form, in this wretched world, with the ugliness of your lives, with the brutality of your existence, with your everyday conflict. That is all you know; you cling to that and you want that modified. And anybody that helps you to live in that field, you think is a great man; he is a saint; he is a marvellous saviour.

Therefore the speaker says he is not giving you help. If you seek help from the speaker, you are lost. There is no help from anybody, of any type—that is a dreadful thing to realize for oneself. You have to realize the appalling, frightening fact that you, as a human being, have to stand completely on your own feet; there are no scriptures, no leaders, nothing that can save you; you have to save yourself. You know what that does when you realize that fact? It *is* a fact. When you actually realize that fact, either you sink further in your corruption, or that very fact gives you tremendous energy to break through the network of the psychological structure of society—break through, shattering everything. And then you will never seek help, because you are free.

A free man, a man who is not frightened, who has a clear mind, whose heart is vital, strong, energetic—he does not want help. And we, you and I, have to stand alone completely, totally, with no help from anybody. You have sought help politically, religiously from the gurus, socially in every way; they have all betrayed you. There have been revolutions—political and economic revolutions, communism, social revolutions. They are not the answers; they cannot help you, because they will bring more tyranny, more slavery.

It is only when you demand complete freedom and sustain that freedom that you will find, through an operational approach, reality, and it is that reality that will set man free—nothing else. And it is one of the most difficult things to realize that you have to stand completely alone, entirely by yourself.

It is only the man who is free who can co-operate. And it is the man who is free, who says: I will not co-operate. Co-operation, as it is generally understood, implies co-operating around a person, around an idea, or for a Utopia, around the authority of a person, or the authority of an idea as the State. If you observe that kind of co-operation, it is not co-operation at all, it is mutual benefit; and when the authority changes, you change in order to derive your benefit from that; so it is a compulsive form of adjustment.

We are talking about co-operation that is entirely different, because man must co-operate. We cannot live without co-operation. Life is relationship, life is co-operation. You and I cannot properly exist without co-operation. But to co-operate there must be freedom. You must be free and I must be free to co-operate. Freedom does not mean doing what we like: being ruthless and all the rest of the stupid reaction connected with that word. It is only the man that is free to love, who has no jealousy, hate, who wants nothing for himself, for his family, for his race, for his group, it is only the man that is free and knows the full significance of love and beauty, who can co-operate.

So what is necessary is to understand this freedom. Thought does not bring about this freedom. Thought is never free. Thought is merely a reaction to accumulated knowledge as memory, as experience; therefore it can never free man. And yet everything that we do—every action, every motive, every urge—is based on thought. So one has to see for oneself the significance of thought, where it is necessary and where it is poison. Mutation can only come about when the mind is totally empty of all thought. It is like the womb: a child is conceived in the womb, because the womb is empty, and out of that a new birth is given. In the same way, the mind must be empty, it is only in emptiness that a new thing can take place—a totally new thing, not a thing that has continued through millennia.

So the question is then: how to empty the mind? Not the system; when I use the word *how*, it is not "do these things and you will empty the mind." There is no system, there is no formula. You have to see the truth of that: that mutation is absolutely necessary for the salvation of·man, for you and me, for our salvation, for our freedom, to be completely free from sorrow, from the agony of life.

You must have a mutation, a mind that is completely different, that is not the product of environment, of society, of reaction, of knowledge, of experience—all those do not bring about innocence, do not bring about freedom; they do not give this vast sense of space in the mind. It is only in that space that the movement of mutation takes place. And it is only that mutation that can save man, because it is that mutation that brings about the individual.

We are not individuals. We have names, separate names. You have a separate body; perhaps, if you are lucky enough, you have a bank account; otherwise, you are not an individual inwardly, psychologically. You belong to the race, to the community, to tradition, to the past, and therefore you have ceased to be creative. You have ceased to be aware of the immensity of the width and the depth and the beauty of life.

Because we are not individuals, we do not know what it means to love. We know only that love that contains jealousy, hate, envy, and all the mischief that thought can bring about. Do observe, if you will, your own so-called affection; observe yourself, your own affection for your wife and your family. There is not a spark of love; it is a unit of corruption, of attachment, of pain, of jealousy, of ambition, of domination. You may beget children, but in that there is no love; it is pleasure. And where there is pleasure, there is pain. And a man who would understand this thing called *love* must first understand what it is to be free.

Then there is the question of sex, which is a great problem in the world. You may be out of it, because of your age or because you have forced yourself. You have no sexual life, because you want to find god. I am afraid you won't find god. God wants a free man, a man who has lived, who has suffered, who is free. So you have to understand this question of sex.

Please listen to what the speaker says. You may not go completely to the very end of the journey, but listen. Listen without condemning, without justifying, without comparing, without bringing all the memories into operation. Just listen freely, happily. Because, if you know how to listen, then you will know when the mind is empty. There is nothing that you can do to bring about that emptiness. Every action on your part is the action of the past, of thought, of time, and time is not going to bring you that freedom. But listen, actually enjoy listening to the sound of a bird, the single sound, each sound separate, distinct, vital, clear; listen to that crow; listen to the speaker completely—to each word, each statement without interpreting, without translating. Just listen. And out of that listening you will have the energy; out of that listening you will act completely, totally.

We do not listen. There are too many noises about us; inside us, there is too much talk, too much questioning, too much demanding, too many urges, compulsions. We have so many things and we never listen to any one of them completely, totally, to the very end. And if you would kindly so listen, you will see that, in spite of yourself, the mutation, that emptiness, that transformation, the perception of what is true, comes into being. You don't have to do a thing, because what you do will interfere, because you are greedy, you are envious, you are full of hate, ambition, and all the mischief that thought can make.

So if you can listen happily, effortlessly, then perhaps in the quiet, deep silence you will know what is truth. And it is only that truth that liberates, and nothing else. That is why you must stand completely alone. You cannot listen through another; you cannot see with the eyes of another; you cannot think with the thoughts of others. But yet you listen through others, see through the activities, through the saints, through the dictum of others. So if you can put away all these secondary things, the activities of others, and be simple, quiet, and listen, then you will find out.

You know, when you look at a sunset or a lovely face or a beautiful leaf or a flower, when you actually see it, then there is space between you and that flower and that beauty and that loveliness, or between you and the misery and the squalor you see. There is space; you have not created it, it is there. You cannot do anything to make that space wide or narrow, it is there. But we refuse to look through that space simply, quietly, persistently.

Through that space we project our opinions, our ideas, our conclusions, our formulas, and therefore there is no space. That space is covered over with yesterdays, with the memories, with the experiences of yesterday; therefore we never see, we never listen, we are never quiet. So if you will, do listen, not being hypnotized—that would be absurd, that would be too immature—not accepting it, not denying it. We are dealing with your life and not with my life; we are dealing with your sorrows, your miseries, your authorities, your despairs, and the agony and the boredom of life.

As we were saying, there is this question of sex, which has become tremendously important. Why? Look at your own lives. Why? First you have no other free pleasure. You are blocked intellectually; you repeat everlastingly what others have said, from childhood till you die. Your examination, your education, your technological information—all this is repetition, repetition. You are blocked intellectually. You dare not think independently. You don't deny. You are yes-sayers. You are followers; you are worshippers of authority. Therefore you are blocked intellectually, and therefore you have only one thing where you are free, original: sex.

Then emotionally, you are not free to express. There too, you are blocked, hindered, contained. You never enjoy the sunset, you never see the tree, nor are you with the tree, in full enjoyment, in the full beauty of the tree. So, emotionally, intellectually, you are starved, cut off, and beauty means nothing to you—nothing. Otherwise, this country would be different. You have divorced religion from beauty. You will never sit up of an evening, quietly looking at the stars, the moon, and the light on the water; you have the radio, television, books, the cinema—anything but being alone with yourself to enjoy that which is about you. So emotionally, aesthetically, deep down you are completely blocked. So you have only one thing left that is your own, original, and that is sex.

And when sex becomes the only thing, it creates havoc in one's life. And that too becomes repetitive, and that too leads to various forms of domination, compulsion, the agony of relationship. That too leads to brutality, to dulling the mind—this repetitive pleasure. So there is no love; there is no beauty in our life, no emotional freedom. And so the thing is left that is called sex.

Then there is no discovery, for yourself, of reality. Because religions have made you followers, not investigators, not explorers, not the people who will discover. You are merely people who repeat endlessly, go to the church or to the temple, or deny and merely live superficially. So religion actually has no meaning, except when you are in a state of fear, disease, or when you want some kind of comfort.

Please listen, don't get bored. This is your life. You have to face these things. And ultimately there is that creation—not of children—that creation that is beyond time and measure, that makes all things new all the time because it is out of time. But we are always seeking new expressions in the world of art, in the world of aesthetics. New expressions—that is all we are concerned with. We are not concerned with creation.

So those are the many problems that confront you and you have to find out the right answer for yourself. And there is the right answer, which is: that there must be complete freedom for you, complete freedom from this sociological structure, the psychological structure of society, which is fear, greed, envy, ambition, the seeking of power, the seeking of position, depending on money. The corruption of society—one has to be free of that. And yet one has to live in this world vitally, strongly, energetically. And to do that, you have to work; you have to work inwardly, ruthlessly, to strip yourself of all the debris of society, of all the corruption of society. When you realize that you have to do it, for yourself, completely, and nobody is going to help you, you have a tremendous energy. Then all your attention is given to that; then you have a mind, a heart that is tremendously alive, active.

So self-knowing is operational; it is not a question of belief; it functions, it operates if you go after it steadily, day after day. Out of self-knowing comes awareness—that is, to be aware of the birds, of the trees, of the squalor, of the dirt, of the beauty, of the colour, of everything about you outwardly. Because the outward movement brings you the inward movement. You cannot ride on the inward without understanding the outward movement. They are one; they are a unitary process just like a tide on the sea, that goes out and comes in. And you must ride on that tide without effort. You can ride on that tide without effort when you observe and when you listen to all the intimations of thought and the implications of your being, when you just listen. It does not demand analysis, introspection—that is deadly. All that it demands is that you look, that you listen, and that you keep that space between the observer and the thing observed. If you keep that space completely empty, there is neither the observer nor the observed; there is only movement.

And out of this self-knowing, there comes freedom that nobody, no god, no saint, no society can give you. You must have this freedom. Because otherwise, the churches with their organized belief and entertainment are going to take over, and you will live mechanically, stupidly, worthlessly. And from this freedom comes that state of mind when the brain is highly sensitive, because it has understood every movement of thought, every wave of feeling— because thought and feeling are not separate things; it is a whole process. And out of that understanding, out of that freedom, the mind is made young, fresh, and innocent. It is only out of this emptiness that mutation comes, and from that alone can there be salvation for man. It is only when the mind has completely undergone this tremendous mutation out of time—not within the limits of society but completely outside society, and not by becoming a monk; that is too immature—when the mind has understood the whole fabric of society, which is yourself, that out of that understanding comes this extraordinary sense of aloneness.

Then you are completely, indissolubly alone. And only then, in that state of complete aloneness, does that movement, which is the beginning and end of all things, come into being. That is religion and nothing else. In that state, there is love; there is compassion and infinite pity. And in that state, there is neither sorrow nor pleasure, but a life that is vitally living, strong, vital, clear.

Saanen, 14 July 1964

THE OTHER DAY I was talking about the necessity of freedom, and by that word *freedom* I do not mean a peripheral or fragmentary freedom at certain levels of one's consciousness. I was talking about being totally free—free at the very root of one's mind, in all one's activities, physical, psychological, and parapsychological. Freedom implies a total absence of problems, does it not? Because when the mind is free it can observe and act with complete clarity; it can be what it is without any sense of contradiction. To me, a life of problems—whether economic or social, private or public—destroys and perverts clarity. And one needs clarity. One needs a mind that sees very clearly every problem as it arises, a mind that can think without confusion, without conditioning, a mind that has a quality of affection, love—which has nothing whatever to do with emotionalism or sentimentality.

To be in this state of freedom—which is extremely difficult to understand, and requires a great deal of probing into—one must have an undisturbed, quiet mind, a mind that is functioning totally, not only at the periphery, but also at the centre. This freedom is not an abstraction, it is not an ideal. The movement of the mind in freedom is a reality, and ideals and abstractions have nothing whatsoever to do with it. Such freedom takes place naturally, spontaneously—without any sort of coercion, discipline, control, or persuasion—when we understand the whole process of the arising and the ending of problems. A mind that has a problem, which is really a disturbance, and has escaped from that problem, is still crippled, bound; it is not free. For the mind that does not resolve every problem as it arises, at whatever level—physical, psychological, emotional—there can be no freedom and therefore no clarity of thought, of outlook, of perception.

Most human beings have problems. I mean by a problem the lingering disturbance created by one's inadequate response to a challenge—that is, by the incapacity to meet an issue totally, with one's whole being—or by the indifference that results in the habitual acceptance of problems and just putting up with them. There is a problem when one fails to confront each issue and go to the very end of it, not tomorrow or at some future date, but as it arises, every minute, every hour, every day.

Any problem at any level, conscious or unconscious, is a factor that destroys freedom. A problem is something that we don't understand completely. One's problem may be pain, physical discomfort, the death of someone, or the lack of money; it may be the incapacity to discover for oneself whether god is a reality, or merely a word without substance. And there are the problems of relationship, both private and public, individual as well as collective. Not to understand the whole of human relationship does breed problems; and most of us have these problems—from which psychosomatic diseases arise—crippling our minds and hearts. Being burdened with these problems, we turn to various forms of escape: we worship the state, accept authority, look to someone else to resolve our problems, plunge into a useless repetition of prayers and rituals, take to drink, indulge in sex, in hate, in self-pity, and so on.

So we have carefully cultivated a network of escapes— rational or irrational, neurotic or intellectual—that enable us to accept and therefore put up with all the human problems that arise. But these problems inevitably breed confusion, and the mind is never free.

❖

THAT IS WHY I have said from the very beginning that freedom is a necessity. Even Karl Marx—the god of the communists—wrote that human beings must have freedom. To me, freedom is absolutely necessary—freedom at the beginning, in the middle, and at the end—and that freedom is denied when I carry a problem over to the next day. This means that I have not only to discover how the problem arises, but also how to end it completely, surgically, so that there is no repetition, no carrying over of the problem, no feeling that I will think about it and find the answer tomorrow. If I carry the problem over to the next day, I have provided the soil in which the problem takes root, and then the pruning of that problem becomes still another problem. Therefore I have to operate so drastically and immediately that the problem comes completely to an end.

❖

TO ME, AS I SAID, freedom is of the highest importance. But freedom cannot possibly be understood without intelligence, and intelligence can come about only when one has completely understood for oneself the causation of problems. The mind must be alert, attentive, it must be in a state of super sensitivity, so that every problem is resolved as it comes along. Otherwise there is no real freedom; there is a fragmentary, peripheral freedom that has no value at all. It is like a rich man saying he is free. Good god! He is a slave to drink, to sex, to comfort, to a dozen things. And the poor man who says, "I am free because I have no money"—he has other problems. So freedom, and the maintenance of that freedom, cannot be a mere abstraction; it must be the absolute demand on your part as a human being, because it is only when there is freedom that you can love. How can you love if you are ambitious, greedy, competitive?

Varanasi, 26 November 1964

WE ONLY KNOW space when there is the observer, the centre, the object, that creates the space. A piece of furniture creates the space around it—so also a wall, a house—and that is the only space you know: the space that you observe with your eyes when you look out from the earth to the moon, to the stars.

So we are going to inquire into this problem of space without the object. And only in that space is freedom; that space without the object is freedom. In inquiring into space and freedom we are also going to discover for ourselves what is love. Because without love there is no freedom. Love is not sentimentality, love is not emotionality. Love is not being in an emotional state, nor is it devotional.

So we are going to find out for ourselves. To find out, we must create space in the mind. We must empty the mind, obviously, so as to give space: not space in a limited field of thought, but space without limit and space within—if we can so divide it—that is, space in the mind and in the heart; otherwise there is no love, no freedom. And without love and freedom man is doomed. You may live very comfortably on the fifteenth floor of a sky-scraper or live most miserably in a filthy little village, but you will be doomed unless there is this extraordinary, limitless space within the mind and the heart, within the whole of your being.

Madras, 16 December 1964

So we are going to ask ourselves whether it is at all possible for the human mind, which is so bound, which is the result of two million years of time and space and distance, which is the result of so many pressures—whether it is possible for such a mind to bring about a mutation out of time and therefore on the instant. And to inquire into this question one must demand freedom, because you cannot inquire if you are tethered. You must have a free mind, a mind that is not afraid, a mind that has no belief, a mind that does not project its own conditioning, its own hopes, its own longings.

So it is only through inquiry that one is going to find out, and to inquire one must have freedom. Most of us have lost—probably we never had—this energy to inquire. We would rather accept, we would rather go along the old path, but we do not know how to inquire. The scientist in his laboratory inquires. He is searching, looking, asking, questioning, doubting, but outside the laboratory he is just like anybody else, he has stopped inquiring! And to inquire into oneself requires not only freedom but an astonishing sense of perception, of seeing.

You know, it is comparatively easy to go to the moon and beyond—as they have proved. But it is astonishingly difficult to go within. And to go within endlessly, the first thing needed is freedom—freedom not from something, but the act of freedom that is independent of motive and revolt. When freedom becomes a revolt it is merely a reaction to the condition it exists in; it is revolting from something and therefore it is not free. I can revolt against the present society. The present society may be stupid, corrupt, inept, ineffective; I can revolt, but that revolt is merely a reaction—as communism is a reaction against capitalism. So this revolt merely puts me in a position modified along the same pattern. So we are not talking of revolt that is a reaction, but we are talking of freedom that is not from something.

I do not know if you have ever felt this nature of freedom—not calculated, not induced—when you suddenly feel that you have no burden, no problem, and your mind is tremendously alive and your whole body—your heart and your nerves, everything—is intense, vibrating, strong. Such freedom is necessary. It is only the free mind that can really inquire, obviously, not a mind that says, "I believe and I will inquire," not a mind that is frightened of what will happen to it through inquiry, and therefore stops inquiring.

Inquiry means a mind that is sane, healthy, that is not persuaded by opinions of its own or of another, so that it is able to see very clearly every minute everything as it moves, as it flows. Life is a movement in relationship that is action. And unless there is freedom, mere revolt has no meaning at all. A really religious man is never in revolt. He is a free man—free, not from nationalism, greed, envy, and all the rest of it; he is just free.

And to inquire, there must be the understanding of the nature and the meaning of fear, because a mind that is afraid at any level of its being cannot obviously be capable of the swift movement of inquiry. You know, because of tradition, because of the weight of authority, especially in India, people are everlastingly boasting of seven thousand years of culture and are very proud of it! And these people who talk everlastingly about this culture, probably have nothing to say, and that is why they are talking about it. Such a mind that is caught in the weight of tradition and authority is not a free mind. One must go beyond civilization and culture. And it is only such a mind that is capable of inquiry and the discovery of what is truth—and no other mind. The traditional mind can talk about what is truth and have theories about it endlessly, but to find out requires a mind that is free from all authority and therefore from all fear.

Saanen, 18 July 1965

WE HAVE BEEN talking about the necessity for a fundamental and radical revolution within oneself. It is not a revolution within oneself as an individual that we are talking about—a matter of saving your own particular little soul—but a revolution within oneself as a human being totally related to all other human beings. We may consciously separate ourselves into petty little individualities, but deep down, unconsciously, we are the inherited human experience of all time. And mere superficial changes on the economic or social level, though they may provide a little more comfort and convenience, are not productive of a new society. We are concerned, not only with the human being's transformation of his total nature, but also with bringing about a different society, a good society, and a good society is not possible if there are no good human beings. Good human beings do not flower in prison. Goodness flowers in freedom, not in tyranny, not in one-party systems, whether political or religious.

Freedom is considered by society to be dangerous to society, because in freedom the individual pursues his own particular enterprise. Through his own cleverness, cunning, the individual dominates others who are less enterprising, and so there is generally a feeling, an idea, a judgment that freedom is contrary to a good society. Therefore political tyrannies try to control, religiously as well as economically and socially, the human mind; they penalize the mind, trying to prevent man from thinking freely. In the so-called democratic societies there is greater freedom, obviously, otherwise we would not be sitting here discussing this matter. It would not be allowed in some countries. But freedom is also denied in the democracies when it takes the form of a revolt. Now, we are not talking about revolt in the political sense, but rather of a complete flowering of human goodness, which can alone produce a creative society.

This goodness of the human being can flower only in freedom, in total freedom, and to understand the question of freedom, one has to go into it, not only in terms of the social order, but also in terms of the individual's relationship to society. Society survives through maintaining some semblance of order. If one observes the society in which one lives, whether it be of the left, the right, or the centre, one sees that society demands order, a social relationship in which the individual does not rampantly exploit others. But order is denied because of the very structure, the basic psychological structure of society. Though it may proclaim otherwise, society as we know it is based on competition, greed, envy, on an aggressive pursuit of one's own fulfillment, achievement, and in such a society there can be no real freedom at all, and therefore no order. Society as it is, whether of the left or of the right, is disorder, because it is not concerned with a fundamental transformation of the human mind. This inner transformation or revolution can take place only in freedom—and by freedom I do not mean a reaction, a freedom from something. Freedom from something is a reaction and that is not freedom at all.

If the mind merely frees itself from a certain attitude, from certain ideas, or from certain forms of its own self-expression, in that freedom from something, which is a reaction, it is driven into still another form of assertion, and hence there is no freedom at all. So one has to be very clear what one means by the word *freedom*. I know this problem of freedom has been discussed in a great many books; it has given rise to philosophies, to religious ideas and concepts, and to innumerable political expressions. But living as we do in a world that is so destructive, so full of sorrow, misery, and confusion, and being so ridden by our own problems, by our own frustrations, despairs, unless you and I—as human beings in total relationship with other human beings—find out for ourselves what freedom is, there can be no flowering of goodness. Goodness is not a mere sentimental word, it has an extraordinary significance, and without it I do not see how one can act without reaction in which there is misery, fear, and despair.

So I think it is necessary for the human mind to understand totally this question of what goodness is. The word *goodness* is not the fact, the word is not the thing, and we should be extremely watchful not to be caught in that word and its definition. Rather we must be, or understand, the state that is goodness. Goodness cannot flower and flourish except in freedom. Freedom is not a reaction, it is not freedom from something, nor is it a resistance or a revolt against something. It is a state of mind, and that state of mind that is freedom cannot be understood if there is no space. Freedom demands space.

There is in the world less and less space; towns are getting more and more crowded. The explosion of population is denying space to each one of us. Most of us live in a little room surrounded by innumerable other rooms, and there is no space except perhaps when we wander into the country, far away from towns, smoke, dirt, and noise. In that there is a certain freedom, but there cannot be inward freedom if there is no inward space. Again, the word *space* is different from the fact, so may I suggest that you don't seize upon that word and get caught in trying to analyze or define it. You can easily look up the word in a dictionary and find out what the dictionary says about space.

Now, can we put to ourselves the question: "What is space?" and remain there, not trying to define the word, not trying to feel our way into it, or to inquire into it, but rather to see what it means non-verbally? Freedom and space go together. To most of us, space is the emptiness around an object—around a chair, around a building, around a person, or around the contours of the mind.

Please just listen to what is being said, don't agree or disagree, because we are about to go into something rather subtle and difficult to express in words, but we must go into it if we are to understand what freedom is.

Most of us know space only because of the object. There is an object, and around it there is what we call space. There is this tent, and within and around it there is space. There is space around that tree, around that mountain. We know space only within the four walls of a building, or outside the building, or around some object. Similarly, we know space inwardly only from the centre, which looks out at it. There is a centre, the image—and again, the word *image* is not the fact—and around this centre there is space; so we know space only because of the object within that space.

Now is there space without the object, without the centre from which you as a human being are looking? Space, as we know it, has to do with design, structure; it exists in the relationship of one structure to another structure, one centre to another centre. Now, if space exists only because of the object, or because the mind has a centre from which it is looking out, then that space is limited, and therefore in that space there is no freedom. To be free in a prison is not freedom. To be free of a certain problem within the four walls of one's relationships—that is, within the limited space of one's own image, one's own thoughts, activities, ideas, conclusions—is not freedom.

Please, may I once again suggest that through the words of the speaker you observe the limited space that you have created around yourself as a human being in relationship with another, as a human being living in a world of destruction and brutality, as a human being in relationship to a particular society. Observe your own space, see how limited it is. I do not mean the size of the room in which you live, whether it is small or big—that is not what I am talking about. I mean the inner space that each one of us has created around his own image, around a centre, around a conclusion. So the only space we know is the space that has an object as its centre.

I don't know if I am making myself clear. I am trying to say that as long as there is a centre around which there is space, or a centre that creates space, there is no freedom at all. And when there is no freedom, there is no goodness nor the flowering of goodness. Goodness can flower only when there is space—space in which the image, the centre, is not.

Let me put it another way. You know, it is the very nature of a good, healthy, strong mind, to demand freedom, not only for itself but for others. But that word *freedom* has been translated in various ways, religious, economic, and social. In India it has been translated in one way, and here in Switzerland another. So let us go into the question of what is freedom for a human being. Isolating oneself in a monastery, or becoming a wandering monk, or living in some fanciful ivory tower—surely that is not freedom at all. Nor is it freedom to identify oneself with a particular religious or ideological group. So let us inquire into what is freedom, and how there can be freedom in every relationship.

Now, to understand freedom in relationship, one must go into this question of what is space, because the minds of most of us are small, petty, limited. We are heavily conditioned—conditioned by religion, by the society in which we live, by our education, by technology; we are limited, forced to conform to a certain pattern, and one sees that there is no freedom within that circumscribed area. But one demands freedom—complete freedom, not just partial freedom. Living in a prison cell for twenty-four hours a day, and going occasionally into the prison yard to walk around there— that is not freedom. As a human being living in the present society, with all its confusion, misery, conflict, torture, one demands freedom, and this demand for freedom is a healthy, normal thing. So living in society—living in relationship with your family, with your property, with your ideas—what does it mean to be free? Can the mind ever be free if it hasn't got limitless space within itself— space not created by an idea of space, not created by an image that has a certain limited space around itself as the centre? Surely, as a human being one has to find out the relationship that exists between freedom and space. What is space? And is there space without the centre, without the object that creates space?

Are you following all this? It is very important to find out for ourselves what space is. Otherwise there can be no freedom and we shall always be tortured, we shall always be in conflict with each other, and we shall only revolt against society, which has no meaning at all. Merely to give up smoking, or to become a beatnik, or god knows what else, has no meaning, because those are all just forms of revolt within the prison.

Now, we are trying to find out if there is such a thing as freedom that is not a revolt—freedom that is not an ideational creation of the mind, but a fact. And to find that out, one must inquire profoundly into the question of space. A petty little bourgeois, middle-class mind—or an aristocratic mind, which is also petty—may think it is free, but it is not free, because it is living within the limits of its own space, the confining space created by the image in which it functions. Is that clear? So you cannot have order without freedom, and you cannot have freedom without space. Space, freedom and order—the three go together, they are not separate. A society of the extreme left hopes to create order through dictatorship, through the tyranny of a political party, but it cannot create order, economically, socially, or in any other way, because order requires the freedom of man within himself—not as an individual saving his petty, dirty little soul, but as a human being who has lived for two million years or more, with all the vast experience of mankind.

Order is virtue, and virtue or goodness cannot flower in any society that is always in contradiction with itself. Outside influences—economic adjustment, social reform, technological progress, going to Mars, and all the rest of it—cannot possibly produce order. What produces order is inquiry into freedom—not intellectual inquiry, but doing the actual work of breaking down our conditioning, our limiting prejudices, our narrow ideas, breaking down the whole psychological structure of society, of which we are part. Unless you break through all that, there is no freedom, and therefore there is no order. It is like a small mind trying to understand the immensity of the world, of life, of beauty. It cannot. It can imagine, it can write poems about it, paint pictures, but the reality is different from the word, different from the image, the symbol, the picture. Order can come about only through the awareness of disorder. You cannot create order—please do see this fact. You can only be aware of disorder, outwardly as well as inwardly. A disordered mind cannot create order, because it doesn't know what it means. It can only react to what it thinks is disorder by creating a pattern that it calls "order," and then conforming to that pattern. But if the mind is conscious of the disorder in which it lives— which is being aware of the negative, not projecting the so-called positive—then order becomes something extraordinarily creative, moving, living. Order is not a pattern that you follow day after day. To follow a pattern that you have established, to practise it day after day, is disorder—the disorder of effort, of conflict, of greed, of envy, of ambition, the disorder of all the petty little human beings who have created and been conditioned by the present society.

Now, can one become aware of disorder—aware of it without choosing, without saying, "This is disorder, and that is order"? Can one be choicelessly aware of disorder? This demands extraordinary intelligence, sensitivity, and in that choiceless awareness there is also a discipline that is not mere conformity.

Am I driving too hard? Am I putting too many ideas in one basket, as it were, presenting them all at the same moment?

You see, for most of us, discipline—whether we like it or not, whether we practise it or not, whether we are conscious or unconscious of it—is a form of conformity. All the soldiers in the world—those poor, miserable human beings, whether of the left or of the right—are made to conform to a pattern, because there are certain things which that they are supposed to do. And although the rest of us are not soldiers trained to destroy others and protect ourselves, discipline is nevertheless imposed on us by environment, by society, by the family, by the office, by the routine of our everyday existence, or we discipline ourselves.

When one examines the whole structure and meaning of discipline, whether it is imposed discipline or self-discipline, one sees that it is a form of outward or inward conformity or adjustment to a pattern, to a memory, to an experience. And we revolt against that discipline. Every human mind revolts against the stupid kind of conformity, whether established by dictators, priests, saints, gods, or whatever they are. And yet one sees that there must be some kind of discipline in life—a discipline that is not mere conformity, that is not adjustment to a pattern, that is not based on fear, and all the rest of it; because if there is no discipline at all, one can't live. So one has to find out if there is a discipline that is not conformity; because conformity destroys freedom, it never brings freedom into being. Look at the organized religions throughout the world, the political parties. It is obvious that conformity destroys freedom, and we don't have to labour the point. Either you see it, or you don't see it: it is up to you.

The discipline of conformity, which is created by the fear of society and is part of the psychological structure of society, is immoral and disorderly, and we are caught in it. Now, can the mind find out if there is a certain movement of discipline that is not a process of controlling, shaping, conforming? To find that out, one has to be aware of this extraordinary disorder, confusion, and misery in which one lives, and to be aware of it, not fragmentarily but totally and, therefore, choicelessly—that in itself is discipline.

If I am fully aware of what I am doing, if I am choicelessly aware of the movement of my hand, for example, that very awareness is a form of discipline in which there is no conformity. Is this clear? You cannot understand this just verbally, you have actually to do it within yourself. Order can come about only through this sense of awareness in which there is no choice, and which is therefore a total awareness, a complete sensitivity to every movement of thought. This total awareness itself is discipline without conformity; therefore, out of this total awareness of disorder, there is order. The mind hasn't produced order.

To have order, which is the flowering of goodness and of

beauty, there must be freedom, and there is no freedom if you have no space.

Look, I will put a question to you—but don't answer me, please. What is space? Put that question to yourself, not just flippantly, but seriously, as I am putting it to you. What is space? Your mind now knows only the space within the limitations of a room, or the space that an object creates around itself. That is the only space you know. And is there space without the object? If there is no space without the object, then there is no freedom, and therefore there is no order, no beauty, no flowering of goodness. There is only everlasting struggle. So the mind has to discover by hard work, and not just by listening to some words, that there is in fact space without a centre. Once that has been found, there is freedom, there is order, and then goodness and beauty flower in the human mind.

Discipline, order, freedom and space cannot exist without the understanding of time. It is very interesting to inquire into the nature of time—time by the watch, time as yesterday, today, and tomorrow, the time in which you work, and the time in which you sleep. But there is also time that is not by the watch, and that is much more difficult to understand. We look to time as a means of bringing about order. We say, "Give us a few more years and we will be good, we will create a new generation, a marvellous world." Or we talk about creating a different type of human being, one who will be totally this or totally that. So we look to time as a means of bringing about order, but if one observes, one sees that time only breeds disorder.

Saanen, 27 July 1965

WHAT WE ARE going to do now is not a matter of sharing, but both of us are going to inquire; we are going to move together into something that we don't know. Please do not wait for me to tell you, or to share something with you that you do not have; do not wait for me to give you enlightenment or freedom. No one can give you freedom, nor can anyone share it with you. But most of us are used to this attitude of someone giving and another receiving, and it creates a division in life that brings about authority with all its evils. In truth there is not the follower and the one who leads, there is neither the teacher nor the taught, and that is a marvellous thing, if you realize it for yourself. In that there is great beauty, in that there is freedom, in that there is the ending of sorrow, because one has to work, to inquire, to break through, to destroy all that is false, and thereby find out for oneself. Now we are going to inquire into two things that for most of us are of the utmost importance in life: love, and the thing called death. To inquire, to find out, to discover, there must obviously be freedom—not freedom at the end, but freedom right from the beginning. Without freedom you can't look, you can't inquire, you can't move into the unknown. For a mind that would inquire, whether in the complicated field of science, or in the complex and subtle field of human consciousness, there must be freedom. You can't come to it with your knowledge, with your prejudices, with your anxieties and fears, for these factors will shape your perception, they will push you in different directions, and therefore all real inquiry ceases.

Similarly, when we are trying to see what this extraordinary thing means—this thing that we call love—we cannot come to it with our personal prejudices, with our conclusions, with our preconceived notions that it must be this way, or it must be that way; we cannot say that love must be expressed in the family, between husband and wife, or that there is profane love and spiritual love, because all this prevents us from going into the question profoundly, freely, and with a certain breathless pursuit.

So to inquire we need freedom, and therefore we must be aware from the very beginning of how conditioned we are, how prejudiced we are; we must be aware of the fact that we look at life through the desire for pleasure, and thereby prevent ourselves from seeing what actually is. And when we are free of these things, then perhaps we can inquire into this extraordinary thing called love.

We live in this world in a state of relationship—relationship between man and woman, between friends, between ourselves and our ideas, our property, and so on. Life demands relationship, and relationship cannot exist when the mind is isolating itself in all its activities. Please watch this process in yourselves. When there is self-centred activity, there is no relationship. Whether you are sleeping in the same bed with another, or going in a crowded bus, or looking at a mountain, as long as your mind is caught up in self-centred activity, obviously it can only lead to isolation, and therefore there is no relationship.

Now, it is from this turmoil of self-centred activity that most of us begin to inquire into what love is, and this again prevents real inquiry, because all self-centred activity is based on the pursuit of pleasure and the avoidance of pain. As long as we are inquiring from a centre that exists for its own pleasure, our inquiry will be useless and vain. To really inquire, there must be freedom from this self-centred activity—and that is extremely difficult. It requires great intelligence, great understanding, great insight, and therefore one has to have a very good mind, a mind that is not sentimental, not emotional, not carried away by enthusiasm, but a mind that is very clear, aware, sensitive all around. It is only such a mind that can begin to inquire into what we call love.

Rome, 10 April 1966

IF ONE WANTS to discover what that reality is, there must be complete freedom from the conditioning that man lives in, which is propaganda. Every day, from childhood, one is told what god is, what He is not, how to find Him through the Saviour, through the priest, through rituals. Unless one can really, seriously be aware of one's conditioning and throw it off, not eventually, but immediately, there is no way out. As far as one understands, there has always been this idea that god is outside and god is within. I don't personally like to use the word *god*, because it is so heavily burdened. One must find out whether there is such a thing, such a truth, whether there is a reality, a something that is unimaginable, unthinkable, unconditioned.

Questioner: There is space outside and space inside the house.

Krishnamurti: Yes, I took that as an example. The house exists in space; it creates space. Because of the house you know space. You can't think of space without a thinker, and you have to find out if there is a space without the object.

Again, take love. The word is heavily loaded, but we are not using it sentimentally, emotionally, or devotionally. We are using it non-sentimentally. When we say, "I love my country, my wife, my family, my god," or anything else, there is an object to be loved, whether the object is an idea or an entity. When the object moves, love becomes entangled, jealous. We want to know if there is love without the object. Neither beauty, nor space, nor love is the result of an object. This is an enormous investigation. To pursue that subject we must have order—order being freedom in which there is no envy, ambition, greed, or worship of success; otherwise there is disorder, and a disordered mind cannot discover anything.

❖

ALL WE HAVE discussed makes the mind not isolated, but very sharply alone. One must be alone, not in the isolated sense of the monk, however. To be truly alone implies freedom. It's not the aloneness of self-pity and loneliness; it is a marvellous thing to see clearly that you are alone. When everyone around you shouts nationalistic slogans and waves the flag, and you think it's all nonsense, you're alone.

New Delhi, 19 November 1967

To COMMIT ONESELF to freedom and to find out what love is—those are the only two things that matter—freedom and that thing called "love." Without total freedom there cannot possibly be love, and a serious man is committed to these two things only, and to nothing else. Freedom implies—does it not?—that the mind frees itself totally from all conditioning. That is, to uncondition itself—from being a Hindu, a Sikh, a Moslem, a Christian, or a Communist—the mind must be in complete freedom, because this division between man as the Hindu, the Buddhist, the Moslem, the Christian, or the American, the Communist, the Socialist, the Capitalist, and so on, has brought disaster, confusion, misery, wars.

So what is necessary first of all is for the mind to free itself from conditioning. You may say it is not possible. If you say it is not possible, then there is no way out. It is like a man living in a prison and saying, "I cannot get out." All that he can do is decorate the prison, polish it, make it more comfortable, more convenient, limit himself and his activities within the four walls of his own making. There are many who say it is not possible—the whole Communist world says it is not possible, therefore let us condition the mind in a different way, brainwash it first, then condition it according to the Communist system. And the religious people have done exactly the same thing, from childhood they are brainwashed and conditioned to believe they are Hindus, Sikhs, Moslems, Catholics. Religions talk about love and freedom, but they insist on conditioning the mind. So if you say man is not capable of freeing himself from his conditioning, then you have no problem. Then you accept the prison and live in the prison, with the wars, with the confusion, with the conflicts, with the misery, the agony, and the loneliness of life, with its violence, brutality, and hatred, which is what you actually do. But if you say, "It must be possible to uncondition the mind," then we can go into it; then we are together—not some authority leading you to it, not the speaker taking your hand and leading you step by step—because when there is freedom there is no authority. Freedom is at the beginning as well as at the end, and if you accept an authority at the beginning, you will always be a slave at the end. So one has to inquire together in freedom; please do understand this. The speaker is not telling you what to do, not setting himself up as an authority—you have had authorities, all you can stomach, with all their absurdities, with all their immaturities—but if you are inquiring (and there is no authority when you inquire) then we can take the journey together, sharing together, not being led. A real scientist is not committed to any government; he has no nationality; he is not seeking an end. As a pure scientist, he is investigating objectively right to the end, without projecting his personality, his nationality, his ambitions.

So inquire into this question of freedom, not intellectually, but actually, with your blood, with your mind, and with your heart! It is only in freedom that you can live, and only when there is freedom is there peace. Then in that freedom the mind has immense peace to wander, but a mind that is not free, tethered to a belief, tethered to an ambition, tethered to a family or to some petty little god of its own invention, such a mind can never understand the extraordinary beauty or the love that comes out of this freedom. And this freedom can only come about naturally, easily, when we begin to understand conditioning, and you cannot be aware of this conditioning when you are held tightly by the four walls of your particular religion, or by ambitions. To inquire into this conditioning one must first become aware. To be aware: this means to observe, to look, to look at your own thoughts, to look at your beliefs, to look at your feelings. But when we do look, we condemn, or justify, or say "that is natural." We don't look with choicelessness; we are not aware of our conditioning. We are aware of our conditioning with choice, with likes and dislikes of what is pleasurable and what is not pleasurable. But we are not actually aware of our conditioning as it is without any choice at all.

Have you ever observed a tree or a cloud, or a bird sitting on the lawn or on a branch? Have you observed what actually takes place? What actually do you feel when you see a tree or a bird or a cloud? Do you see the cloud or do you see the image you have about that cloud? Do please, find out. You see a bird and you give it a name, or you say, "I don't like that bird," or, "How beautiful that bird is." So when you say these things you are not actually seeing the bird at all; your words, your thoughts—whether you like it or not—prevent you from looking. But there is a choiceless awareness to look at something without all the interference of what you already know. After all, to be in communion with another is only possible when you listen without any acceptance or denial, just listen. In the same way look at yourself as if in a mirror—what you actually are, not what you should be, or what you want to be. We dare not look; if we do look we say, "How ugly I am," or "How angry I am"—this or that. To look, to see and to listen, is only possible when there is freedom from thoughts, emotions, condemnation, and judgment.

Probably you have never looked at your wife or your husband without the image that you have about him or about her. Please observe this in your own life. You have an image of him, or she has an image of you and the relationship is between these two images, and these images have been built up, through many years of pleasure and of wrangles, bitterness, anger, criticism, annoyance, irritation, frustration. And so we look at things through the images that we have built about them. You are listening to the speaker, but you have an image about him, therefore you are listening to the image, and you are not directly in contact with him, nor with anything in life. When one is in direct contact, do you know what happens? Space disappears, the space between two people disappears and therefore there is immense peace—and this is only possible when there is freedom, freedom from the making of images, from the myths, the ideologies, so that you are directly in contact. Then, when you are directly in contact with the actual, there is a transformation.

You know what is happening in the world. People are experimenting, taking drugs, and when you take certain drugs, the space between the observer and the observed disappears. Have you ever watched a bouquet of flowers on a table? If you have looked at it attentively, you will have seen that there is a space between you and the thing observed. The space is time, and the drug chemically removes that space and time, therefore you become extraordinarily sensitive, and being very sensitive, you feel much more, because then you are directly in contact with the flower. But such contact is temporary, you have to go on taking drug after drug. When one observes oneself one sees how narrowly one is conditioned, believing in so many things, like a savage with too many superstitions to be directly in contact with things. But you will see if you are directly in contact, that there is then no observer at all. It is the observer that makes the division.

When one is angry, anger is apparently something different from the entity that says: "I am angry." So anger is different from the observer. But is that so? Is not the observer himself anger? And when this division comes totally to an end, then the observer is the observed and therefore anger is no longer possible. Anger and violence only exist when there is the division between the observer and the observed. It is a very complex question that requires a great deal of inquiry, penetration, insight. It is only when there is freedom from all conflict that there is peace, and out of that peace comes love. But one cannot possibly know that quality of love unless the mind is aware of itself, and has unconditioned itself and therefore is free.

New Delhi, 23 November 1967

WE WERE SAYING the other day that there are fundamentally only two problems for man, for the human: freedom and love. Freedom implies order. But order, social order, is now chaotic, contradictory; it is disorder. As you observe the society in which you live, what you call order is essentially disorder because there is violence. Each human being is in competition with another, there is brutality, there is competition to destroy the other, and so on, which essentially is disorder. War, hate, ambition, are disorder and we accept this disorder as order, don't we? We accept this morality, the social morality, as orderly, but when you observe it very closely it is disorder. I think that is fairly clear, unless one is totally blinded by tradition, by one's own convenience, and so on.

CAN ONE BE aware of that and of whether that awareness will bring about a radical revolution—now! Freedom is not from something—please do understand, we are going through rather difficult things and explanation is never the actual thing; unfortunately we think that by explaining we understand something, but we don't. Explanation is one thing and actuality is another. The word *tree* is not the tree, but we confuse the word with the tree. So freedom, what we call freedom, is freedom from something: freedom from anger, freedom from violence, freedom from this utter despair. And when you are free from something are you actually free? Please do go into it in yourselves, observe it. Or is freedom something entirely different and not from something? Being free from something is a reaction and the reaction can go on repeating itself indefinitely. But the freedom we are talking about is entirely different, the sense of being completely free—not from anything. And this quality of awareness of what is implied in being free from something, awareness of the whole structure of it, will naturally bring about a freedom that is not a reaction.

SO AWARENESS IS this quality of mind that observes without any justification or condemnation, approval or disapproval, like or dislike—it merely observes. And it becomes rather difficult when you are stirred up emotionally, when your security, when your family, when your opinions, judgments, and beliefs are shaken—and they will be shaken. There is nothing whatsoever that is secure; everything is in change and we refuse to accept this change, and hence the battle in ourselves. So when you observe yourself very quietly and the world about you, then out of this observation comes freedom—not the freedom from something. Is this fairly clear?

I do not know if you are meeting this point. "I am afraid of death"; that is something that is going to happen tomorrow, or the day after tomorrow, in time. There is a distance from actuality to what will be. Thought has experienced this state, by observing death; it says: I am going to die. Thought creates the fear of death, and if it does not, is there any fear at all? So is fear the result of thought? Because thought is old, fear is always old. Please follow this carefully. Thought is old, there is no new thought. If you recognize a new thought it is already the old. So what we are afraid of is the repetition of the old; thought projecting into the future what has been. So thought is responsible for fear, and this is so; you can see it for yourself, when you are confronted with something immediately, there is no fear. It is only when thought comes in, then there is fear. So our question is: Is it possible for the mind to live so completely, so totally in the present, that there is neither the past nor the future? It is only such a mind that has no fear. But to understand this you have to understand the structure of thought, memory, time. And without understanding it, not intellectually, not verbally, but actually with your heart, with your mind, there is no freedom. But when there is total freedom then the mind can use thought without creating fear.

So freedom from fear is absolutely necessary. Freedom is absolutely necessary, because if there is no freedom there is no peace, there is no order, and therefore there is no love, and when there is love then you can do what you will. Then there is no sin, then there is no conflict. But to understand freedom and love, one has to understand non-verbally the quality of freedom that comes when disorder is understood. This disorder is understood when you understand the structure and the nature of thought, not according to the speaker, nor according to some psychologist; when you understand according to them, you do not understand yourself, you understand according to some authority. To understand yourself there must be a complete throwing away of all authority. Don't please agree, that agreement is merely verbal, it has no meaning; but see why it is important, because all the authorities, your scriptures, your books, your gurus, your religious leaders have led you to this terrible state of complete despair, loneliness, misery, confusion. You have followed them, at least you have pretended to follow them, and now you have to take the journey by yourself, there is no authority that is going to lead you, lead you to a bliss that is not to be found in any book, in any temple. You have to take the journey entirely by yourself. You can't trust anybody; why should you trust anybody? Why should you trust any authority? You say, "I am confused," "I don't know," "You know, so please tell me." Which means what? You are escaping from your own confusion, and to understand your confusion you cannot look to somebody to help you out of that confusion. That confusion has come into being because of this outward authority. Look at it, it is so clear.

On Freedom and Order
From Krishnamurti on Education, *Chapter 4*

FREEDOM DOES NOT EXIST without order. The two go together. If you cannot have order, you cannot have freedom. The two are inseparable. If you say, "I will do what I like. I will turn up for my meals when I like; I will come to the class when I like"—you create disorder. You have to take into consideration what other people want. To run things smoothly, you have to come on time. If I had come ten minutes late this morning I would have kept you waiting. So I have to have consideration. I have to think of others. I have to be polite, considerate, be concerned about other people. Out of that consideration, out of that thoughtfulness, out of that watchfulness, both outward and inward, comes order and with that order there comes freedom.

You know, soldiers all over the world are drilled every day, they are told what to do, to walk in line. They obey orders implicitly without thinking. Do you know what that does to man? When you are told what to do, what to think, to obey, to follow, do you know what it does to you? Your mind becomes dull, it loses its initiative, its quickness. This external, outward imposition of discipline makes the mind stupid, it makes you conform, it makes you imitate. But if you discipline yourself by watching, listening, being considerate, being very thoughtful—out of that watchfulness, that listening, that consideration for others, comes order. Where there is order, there is always freedom. If you are shouting, talking, you cannot hear what others have to say. You can only hear clearly when you sit quietly, when you give your attention.

Nor can you have order if you are not free to watch, if you are not free to listen, if you are not free to be considerate. This problem of freedom and order is one of the most difficult and urgent problems in life. It is a very complex problem. It needs to be thought over much more than mathematics, geography, or history. If you are not really free, you can never blossom, you can never be good, there can be no beauty. If the bird is not free, it cannot fly. If the seed is not free to blossom, to push out of the earth, it cannot live. Everything must have freedom, including man. Human beings are frightened of freedom. They do not want freedom. Birds, rivers, trees, all demand freedom, and man must demand it too, not in half measures, but completely. Freedom, liberty, the independence to express what one thinks, to do what one wants to do, is one of the most important things in life. To be really free from anger, jealousy, brutality, cruelty—to be really free within oneself—is one of the most difficult and dangerous things.

You cannot have freedom merely for the asking. You cannot say, "I will be free to do what I like." Because there are other people also wanting to be free, also wanting to express what they feel, also wanting to do what they wish. Everybody wants to be free, and yet they want to express themselves—their anger, their brutality, their ambition, their competitiveness, and so on. So there is always conflict. I want to do something and you want to do something and so we fight. Freedom is not doing what one wants, because man cannot live by himself. Even the monk, even the sannyasi is not free to do what he wants, because he has to struggle for what he wants, to fight with himself, to argue within himself. And it requires enormous intelligence, sensitivity, understanding to be free. And yet it is absolutely necessary that every human being, whatever his culture, be free. So you see, freedom cannot exist without order.

Student: Do you mean that to be free there should be no discipline?

Krishnamurti: I carefully explained that you cannot have freedom without order and order is discipline. I do not like to use that word *discipline* because it is laden with all kinds of meaning. Discipline means conformity, imitation, obedience; it means to do what you are told, doesn't it? But, if you want to be free—and human beings must be completely free, otherwise they cannot flower, otherwise they cannot be real human beings—you have to find out for yourself what it is to be orderly, what it is to be punctual, kind, generous, unafraid. The discovery of all that is discipline. This brings about order. To find out you have to examine, and to examine you must be free. If you are considerate, if you are watching, if you are listening, then, because you are free, you will be punctual, you will come to the class regularly, you will study, you will be so alive that you will want to do things rightly.

S: You say that freedom is very dangerous to man. Why is it so?

K: Why is freedom dangerous? You know what society is?

S: It is a big group of people that tells you what to do and what not to do.

K: It is a big group of people that tells you what to do and what not to do. It is also the culture, the customs, the habits of a certain community; the social, moral, ethical, religious structure in which man lives, that is generally called society. Now, if each individual in that society did what he liked, he would be a danger to that society. If you did what you liked here in the school, what would happen? You would be a danger to the rest of the school. Wouldn't you? So people do not generally want others to be free. A man who is really free, not in ideas, but inwardly free from greed, ambition, envy, cruelty, is considered a danger to people, because he is entirely different from the ordinary man. So society either worships him or kills him or is indifferent to him.

S: You said that we must have freedom and order, but how are we to get it?

K: First of all, you cannot depend on others; you cannot expect somebody to give you freedom and order whether it is your father, your mother, your husband, your teacher. You have to bring it about in yourself. This is the first thing to realize, that you cannot ask anything except food, clothes, and shelter from another. You cannot possibly ask, or look to anyone, your gurus or your gods. Nobody can give you freedom and order. So you have to find out how to bring about order in yourself. That is, you have to watch and find out for yourself what it means to bring about virtue in yourself. Do you know what virtue is—to be moral, to be good? Virtue is order. So you have to find out in yourself how to be good, how to be kind, how to be considerate. And out of that consideration, out of that watching, you bring about order and therefore freedom. You depend on others to tell you what you should do, that you should not look out of the window, that you should be punctual, that you should be kind. But if you were to say, "I will look out of the window when I want to look, but when I study I am going to look at the book," you bring order within yourself without being told by others.

S: What does one gain by being free?

K: Nothing. When you talk about what one gains, you are really thinking in terms of merchandise, are you not? I will do this and in return for it, please give me something. I am kind to you because it is profitable for me. But that is not kindliness. So as long as we are thinking in terms of gaining something, there is no freedom. If you say, "If I get freedom, I will be able to do this and that," then it is not freedom. So do not think in terms of utility. As long as we are thinking in terms of using, there is no question of freedom at all. Freedom can only exist when there is no motive. You do not love somebody because he gives you food, clothes, or shelter. Then it is not love.

Freedom and the Field

From Tradition and Revolution, *Dialogue 19,*
Madras, 16 January 1971

I HAVE GOT IT: I see that this *concern* about freedom, freedom which is not a formula, which is not a conclusion, is not freedom. Right? Then the mind says, "If this is not it, then what is freedom?" Then it says, "I do not know."

It sees that in that not-knowing, there is an expectation to know. When I say I do not know what freedom is, there is a waiting and an expectation to find out. That means the mind does not really say it does not know, but is waiting for something to happen.

I see that and I discard that.

So I really do not know.

I am not waiting, expecting. I am not hoping something will happen, some answer will come from an outside agency. I am not expecting a thing. There it is. There is the clue.

I know this is not "it." There is no freedom here. There is reformation but not freedom. Reformation can never bring freedom. Man revolts against the whole idea that he can never be free, that he is condemned to live in this world. It is not intellect that revolts, but the whole organism, the whole perception. Right? Therefore it says that as this is not "it," I do not know what freedom is. I do not expect a thing, I do not hope or try to find what freedom is. I really do not know. That not-knowing is freedom. Knowing is prison. This is logically right.

I do not know what is going to happen tomorrow. Therefore I am free of the past, free of this field.

The knowing of the field is the prison, the not-knowing of the field is also the prison.

Sir, look, I know yesterday. I know what happened yesterday. The knowing of what happened yesterday is the prison.

So the mind that lives in a state of not-knowing is a free mind. Right?

The traditionalists went wrong when they said, "Do not be attached." You see, they denied all relationships. They could not solve the problem of relationships, but they said, "Do not be attached," and so broke away from all relationships. They said, "Be detached," therefore they withdrew into isolation.

To live with the knowledge of this field is prison. And not to know the prison is also not freedom.

And so a mind that lives in the known, is always in prison. That is all.

Can the mind say I do not know, which means the yesterday has ended? It is the knowledge of continuity that is the prison.

Questioner: To pursue this requires ruthlessness.

Krishnamurti: Do not use the word ruthlessness. It requires tremendous delicacy. When I said I really do not know, I really do not know. Full stop. See what it does. It means a real humility, a sense of austerity. Then, yesterday has ended. So the man who has ended yesterday is really beginning again. Therefore he has to be austere. I really do not know; what a marvellous thing that is. I do not know if I may die tomorrow. Therefore there is no possibility of having any conclusion at any time, which means, never to have any burden. The burden is the knowing.

Q: Can one come to this point and stay there?

K: You do not have to stay.

Q: The mind has a way of switching back. Words take you only to a point. There is no room for switching back.

K: Go slowly. Do not put it that way. We see this. We see the man who speaks of detachment, we see the man who invents the atman. We come along and say, "Look, both are wrong. In this field there is no freedom."

Then we ask, "Is there freedom at all?" I say, "I really do not know." It does not mean I have forgotten the past. In the "I do not know," there is no inclusion of the past nor a discarding of the past, nor a utilization of the past.

All that it says is, "In the past there is no freedom." The past is knowledge; the past is accumulation; the past is the intellect. In that there is no freedom.

In asking is there freedom at all, man says, "I really do not know."

Q: But the structure of the brain cells remains.

K: They become extraordinarily flexible. Being flexible they can reject, accept; there is movement.

Q: We see something as action. So far we only know activity. We can never reject activity. It goes on. In laying down bare activity, it ceases to be a barrier to action. The normal day-to-day living is a process that goes on.

K: Are you asking what is action? What is action to a man who does not know? The man who knows is acting from knowledge and his action, his activity is always within the prison, projecting that prison into the future. It is always within the field of the known.

Brockwood Park, 9 September 1972

So HOW IS one to learn what freedom is? Not freedom from oppression, freedom from fear, freedom from all the little things that we worry about, but freedom from the very cause of fear, from the very cause of our antagonism, from the very root of our being in which there is this appalling contradiction, this frightening pursuit of pleasure, and all the gods we have created, with all their churches and priests—you know all the rest of the business. So one has to ask oneself, it seems to me, whether you want freedom at the periphery, or at the very core of your being. And if you want to learn what freedom is at the very source of all existence then you have to learn about thought. If that question is clear, not the verbal explanation, not the idea that you gather from the explanation, but if that is what you feel is the real absolute necessity, then we can travel together. Because if we could understand this then all our questions will be answered.

So one has to find out what learning is. First, I want to learn whether there is freedom from thought—not how to use thought, that is the next question. But can the mind ever be free from thought? What does this freedom mean? We only know freedom from something—freedom from fear, freedom from this or that, from anxiety, from a dozen things. And is there a freedom which is not from anything but freedom *per se*, in itself? And in asking that question is the reply dependent on thought? Or is freedom the non-existence of thought? You understand? And learning means instant perception, therefore learning does not require time. I don't know if you see this. Please, this is really fascinatingly important!

❖

TO LEARN IMPLIES time. To learn a language, a technique, a method, acquiring certain information, knowledge about mechanics and so on, that requires time, several months, several years. Learning the piano, the violin, a language, that is really memorizing, practising, acquiring knowledge, which can be translated into action, and that is all we are concerned with; all human beings are only concerned with that, because that gives them power, position, a means of livelihood, and so on. And I say to myself, learning must be instantaneous, learning is the seeing and the acting, in which there is no seeing and a gap and then acting. That is, time is required to learn a language. Is time required to learn freedom? You understand? Is time required for the mind to see that as long as it functions within the pattern of thought there is no freedom, however expanded, however worthwhile, marvellous the expansion, the content of that expansion is? To see that, does it require time to learn about the truth that freedom is not within that pattern—right? That is, are you going to take time to see the truth of that? You have understood my question? Look, you have explained to me what thought has done in the world, you explained to me that a new kind of pattern, still made by thought, will help to bring about a different behaviour. And your explanation and my acceptance of that explanation, the logical process of it, the verbal communication, the reference to all the words that you have used that are so familiar to me—all that takes time, right? And at the end of that the mind is still not free, is still within that pattern. Are we following each other? And you tell me that to learn what is freedom, is instantaneous, it doesn't require time, time is thought and don't use thought to understand freedom at all. So I say to myself, what are you talking about? I don't understand because I have only one instrument, which is thinking. And I have used it wrongly, rightly, mischievously, or nobly, but that is the only instrument I have. And you tell me, put that instrument aside. Learn not about the activities of thought, which you already know, but learn—which is instantaneous—how to look. Learn what freedom is without time.

Are we following each other? You understand my question? That is, perception is learning and perception doesn't require time, and time is basically the movement of thought, and through thought you cannot learn what freedom is. And to learn about freedom, thought must be completely silent.

Questioner: How can it be silent?

Krishnamurti: Listen. Not how—do you see? The moment you say "how" then you want a method, a practice, which is still within the pattern of thought.

So I have this problem from you: thought has its right place otherwise you and I couldn't communicate with each other. But to learn about communication I have to learn the language, and since you and I both know English we can communicate together, and to learn English takes time. Insight into freedom doesn't take time, and you cannot have insight into freedom if there is the operation of thought, or the movement of thought that says, "I must understand what freedom is"—right? So there is this problem then: I am used to thinking, which is the only instrument I have, and I have been educated, brought up to think, all my conditioning, all my existence is based on that, all my relationship is based on the image that thought has created. And you come along and tell me, "Don't use that instrument, but look, perceive, learn, have an insight." And then I say, "How am I to have an insight if my mind is so heavily conditioned, so burdened with all the things of thought, how am I to be free of that in order to see the other?" Right? You have put the wrong question. If you say, "I must be free of this"—which is the mechanical process of thinking—you have stated a wrong question because you are not learning about the new. You still are concerned with the old and where you are concerned with the old you will remain with the old. I wonder if you get all this?

So the real question is: Can the mind, knowing the whole content of the old, not be concerned with it now, because we are inquiring into something in a totally different dimension? And this inquiry demands freedom, not that you should understand the old and bring the old over, or control the old, or subjugate the old, or suppress the old, but move away completely from the old and learn about the new, which doesn't take time. Right, have you got it? It all sounds contradictory and absurd—it isn't.

Q: Surely thought must precede perception? We can't stop thinking.

K: That is just it. You can't stop thinking.

Q: It isn't something that falls out of the sky onto a blank.

K: I understand this. If you want to see something new what do you do? You are inventing, you are an inventor. You know all the old business, you want to find something new, totally new. What do you do? Keep on with the old? The old with which you are familiar, you know what the old is, the whole mechanism of the old. And if you carry that over you can't find anything new. So what do you do? You must leave the old. There must be a gap between the old and something new that may come into being. There must be a gap. And that gap takes place when you see the whole significance of the old—that the old cannot possibly give birth to the new. So we all want the new because we are fed up with the old, bored, you know what the old is, and wanting the new we don't know how to break the chain. So there are gurus, teachers, and all the absurd people who say, "I'll teach you how to break the chain." And their breaking the chain is still within the pattern of thought—right? They say, "Do this, don't do that, follow this, think of that"—they are still caught within the system of thought. Now if you see that, if you have an insight into that, to have an insight into that doesn't require time. I don't know if you see that. You see that instantly, how absurd this whole religious structure is, all the organization around it, the popes, the bishops—you follow?—the absurdity of all that. Grown up people playing with childish things. If you have an insight into that it is finished. Then you ask, "How am I to have an insight?" Which means you haven't actually listened. You are still holding on to your old skirts of the churches, beliefs and ideologies, and you say, "I can't let go because I am afraid." "What will my neighbour think?" "I will lose my job." So you don't want to listen, so that is the problem, not how to acquire perception, not how to come by insight, but rather that you don't listen to the danger of the whole thing that thought has built. And to have the insight you have to listen, you have to let go and listen. If you listen to that pigeon—which means to listen without naming, without condemning, to really listen—then when you listen you have the insight, right?

So freedom—absolute freedom, not relative freedom—absolute freedom is only possible when the mind understands thought and its place and the freedom of thought, right? Now where are we after saying all this? Because after all, you and I are learning together. You have spent time to come here, energy and money and all the rest of it, and are you learning or merely memorizing? If you are merely memorizing then you repeat what others have said, therefore you become secondhand human beings. Instead of repeating Lao-Tse, the Buddha, Marx, or whatever, now you'll repeat what K is talking about, but you will still be secondhand; whereas if you learn you will be out of that class altogether, away from all that rubbish.

So where are we? Is there an insight into freedom, insight into freedom from thought? And when there is that insight into freedom from thought then in that freedom thought can function logically, sanely, objectively, non-personally. So how am I, so heavily conditioned, who use thought from morning until evening, during my sleep, dreaming, waking—all the time the mind is employed with thought—how is that mind to have an insight into the freedom in which there is no thought? Please put that question to yourself. And when you have put that question to yourself, is thought answering that question? If thought is answering that question then there is no freedom, but when you put that question, really seriously, intensely, passionately, when you want to find out, then you will see there is freedom that you have not sought. The seeking is the movement of thought.

Saanen, 1 August 1976

Questioner: Do you have to be alone to be free, and in that freedom what is relationship with another human being? Cannot there be freedom in human relationship?

Krishnamurti: Now the question is: Does freedom imply aloneness? Right, that was the question that was asked? The dictionary meaning of the word *alone* is, "all made into one, all one." Now how can there be freedom if there is self-centred activity, which prevents aloneness? Right? If I am concerned everlastingly about myself—my problems, my worries, my wife, my cooking, you know, worried, worried, concerned all about that, occupied—if my mind is occupied with many things, which is self-centred, there cannot be aloneness, can there? So freedom is a non-occupied mind. A mind that is occupied, it doesn't matter with what—with god, with worries, with money, with sex, with pleasure, occupied, which most of us are, we are occupied with something or other—as long as there is this occupation with something there cannot be freedom, obviously.

And when there is that freedom, the questioner asks: What then is relationship in that freedom—if you have such freedom? First have that freedom and find out. But without having that freedom we are asking, what relationship is. I am not trying to belittle it. But the fact is, our minds are occupied with chattering, with vanity, arrogance, all kinds of things, self-pity and so on. Can that mind be free of all that? And when it is free, isn't it alone?

Because it is something totally different from the other whose mind is occupied. I wonder if you see that. Right?

So if a man, a human being, is free from this tremendous occupation that is going on, then what is his relationship? Can a human being find that out? To find that out he must unburden himself of all the content of occupation, the content of his consciousness, which then is freedom. Then what takes place if you are free and another is not? You, as a human being, may be free from all worries and all occupation, and another is not, then what is the relationship between the two of you? What is the responsibility of the man who is free to another who is not?

Now you wanted to talk about love. What place has freedom, which is a man who is not occupied, burdened with tremendous occupation, problems and all the rest of it—what is his relationship with another who is not free? Is there love in that relationship? Or is it only then that there *is* love? Now look, what do we mean by the word *love?* Be careful! To separate the word from the thing, what is that thing when you separate the word from the feeling? You love another—what is it that you love? Please, you love another, don't you—your wife, your husband, your girl, your boy, or whatever you call it—you love. What does that word mean to you when you use that word? Has love a motive? Please, don't shake your head, for us it has. Because you give another sex, or give him comfort, or cook his meal, or depend on him, possess him, dominate him, push him around, or her around—possession, attachment, all that is implied in that word. Jealousy, anger, hatred, a sense of anxiety, fear, because you may lose that person, all that arises, and that we call love. Right? We are not being cynical, we are just looking at facts.

❖

TO DISCOVER WHAT it means to love, mustn't one be free of all that? Free of attachment—let's take that for the moment. When one is attached, what are you attached to? Suppose one is attached to a table, what does that attachment imply? Pleasure, sense of possession and the utility of it, the feeling that it is a marvellous table so I must hold it, and so on and so on. So when a human being is attached to another, what is going on? If someone is attached to you, what is the feeling of the other who is attached to you? In that attachment there is pride of possession, a sense of domination, fear of losing it, losing that person, therefore jealousy, and therefore greater attachment, greater possessiveness—right? And jealousy, anxiety, all that comes up. Now if there is no attachment does it mean no love, no responsibility? You understand my question? For most of us love means this terrible conflict between human beings, and so relationship becomes a perpetual anxiety—you know all this, I don't have to tell you—and that we call love. And to escape from this terrible strain of what we call love, we have all kinds of entertainment: television or—forgive me if I use the words—religious entertainment. Marvellous! We quarrel and go off to church, or the temple, and come back and begin again. So all this is going on all the time.

So can man, or woman, be free of all this? Or is that impossible? If it is not possible then our life is perpetually a state of anxiety, and from that all kinds of neurotic attitudes, beliefs, actions take place. Now is it possible to be free of attachment, which implies a great deal? Is it possible for a human being to be free of attachment and yet feel responsible?

Now to be free of attachment doesn't mean its opposite—detachment. You follow? It is very important to understand this. When we are attached we know the pain of attachment, the anxiety of it, and we say, "For god's sake I must detach myself from all this horror." So the battle of detachment begins, the conflict. Whereas if you observe, are aware of the fact and the word—the word attachment and freedom from that word, which is the feeling—then observe that feeling without any judgment—observe it—then you will see that out of that total observation there is quite a different movement taking place that is neither attachment or detachment. You understand this? Are you doing it as we are talking, or are you just listening to a lot of words? You know you are attached, don't you?—it doesn't matter to what, to something or other, to a belief, to a prejudice, to a conclusion, to a house, to a person, to some ideal, tremendously attached. Attachment gives great security, which is an illusion—right? It is an illusion to be attached to something because that something may go away. So what you are attached to is the image that you have built about that. I wonder if you get it.

Can you be free of this attachment so that there is a responsibility that is not a duty? Then what is love when there is no attachment? You understand my question? Look: if you are attached to a nationality, you worship isolation of nationality, which is a form of glorified tribalism; you are attached to it. What does that do? It breaks things up, doesn't it? I am tremendously attached to my nationality as a Hindu, and you are attached to your nationality: German, French, Italian, English. We are separate. And therefore the wars and all the complexity of all that goes on. Now if there is no attachment, you have no attachment, what takes place? Is that love? I wonder if you are getting it? Are we understanding each other a little bit?

So attachment separates—right? I am attached to my belief, and you are attached to your belief, therefore there is separation. Just see the consequences of it, the implications of it. So where there is attachment, there is separation, and therefore there is conflict. Where there is conflict there cannot possibly be love. And what is the relationship of a man and a woman, or a man and whatever it is, what is his relationship to another when there is freedom? You understand? Freedom from attachment, all the implications of it. Is that the beginning—I am just using the word *beginning*, don't jump on it—is that the beginning of compassion? You understand? When there is no nationality, and there is no attachment to any belief whatsoever, to any conclusion, to any ideal, then that human being is a free human being. And his relationship with another is out of freedom, isn't it, out of love, out of compassion. I wonder if you are getting all this?

Saanen, 13 July 1978

THIS IDENTIFICATION WITH our bodies, with our experiences, with the house, with the family, with the nation, with a particular ideology or belief has brought about the emphasis on the self, the "me," the ego. And that has cultivated the idea—and I am using the word *idea* in its proper sense—the idea of an individual, that we human beings are separate, distinct individuals apart from everybody else. This emphasis on individuality has created a lot of mischief. It has destroyed families—I don't know if you are aware of that—it has brought about excellence in achievement, in technology, a sense of highest endeavour on the part of a particular human being, the individual, the individual enterprise. Opposed to that there is the whole ideology of totalitarianism. So we have these two opposites. On the one side freedom, so-called freedom, on the other no freedom at all, except for the few. And as one observes throughout the world, the excellence of the individual has brought about certain beneficial results, not only in the technological world, but also in the artistic world. And though the individual thinks he is free, is he free actually? And on the other side of the coin is totalitarianism, where there is no freedom at all, except for the few.

Now what is the truth of this? It is obvious there must be freedom. What do we mean by that word *freedom?* Again let us be very clear that we are asking this question of ourselves, that the speaker isn't asking, you are asking. As we said, there is no speaker here. You and I are the speakers. You and I—this person talking—are inquiring together into this question: on the one side is the enormous importance given to individuality with all its identification, nation, house, family, capitalism, and socialism, whatever it is; and on the other is identification with the ideological society. Society there becomes all important according to the few. And in inquiring into this we must first ask, if I may suggest, what is it we human beings are trying to do? What is it that we human beings—not Mr. So-and-so, Mrs. So-and-so—but as human beings without labels, without nationalities, without all the rubbish that has been pushed down our throats by other people as well as by us down other people's throats, what is it that we human beings are trying to do in this world? What is it that we are seeking, that we are searching, longing for? And one of the questions involved in this is: What is freedom? We think we are free because we can travel, go to America, go anywhere we like if we have money and the inclination.

So what is freedom? Perhaps most of us, at least those who are serious and thoughtful, aware, must inevitably ask this question: What is freedom? Is it freedom to do what you like, as an individual? Is freedom a permissive activity? That is, each one wants to do what he wants to do. If he wants to believe in god, he believes in god. If he wants to pursue and take drugs and sex and all the rest of it, he is free, if he has the money and if he has the inclination and all the rest of it, to go with that. And we have considered this kind of activity freedom: to do what one likes to do, what one wants to do, what one wants to fulfil, or to find identity in freedom. You know all this. So is this freedom? Or is freedom something entirely different? We think of freedom as being free from something, from poverty, from a person you have married whom you don't want any more and are free to divorce and all the rest of it. Free to choose your activity in the business world, or in the psychological world, or free to believe what you want to believe and so on and so on. One is free, one thinks, to choose to become a Catholic, or a Protestant, or not to believe in anything at all. You know all this.

So is that freedom? Please ask yourself this question, not me. You are facing the mirror, looking at yourself, investigating the whole psychological structure of yourself. And our conditioning has been to do what we want to do. And we have never inquired into what it is that urges us to do, either to go left, right, or whatever it is. And as long as there is identity with a nation, with a family, with a husband, with a girl, with this belief, with that dogma, ritual, tradition, is there freedom? You are following all this? You are asking these questions. I am only voicing your inquiry. As we may point out again, we are not authoritative here, there is nobody, as far as the speaker is concerned, with any sense of authority, any sense of superiority. There is no dogmatism, there is no belief. And if the speaker is rather emphatic, it is not an assertive, aggressive expression, it is his natural self.

So we are inquiring if there is freedom in its total sense, not from something to something else, or from something else to something else. We are inquiring into this whole feeling of freedom, if there is such a thing. And as long as the mind, thought, sensation, emotions identify themselves with a particular object, a piece of furniture, a human being, or a belief, is there freedom? Obviously not. The moment you identify yourself with something you are denying freedom. If I, because I like the idea of some supreme being and all the rest of it, identify myself with that and pray to that, worship that, is there freedom at all? So we are discovering that there is no freedom as long as there is an identifying process going on—right?

Please, words are dangerous. Don't, if I may suggest, translate what is being said into your own words, into your own language, into your own opinion, but actually listen to the words we are using, because then we are in direct communication. All right, let me put it this way: language—that is the usage of words, the meaning of the words, the syntax—language drives most of us, right? When you say, "I am a Frenchman," the word is active and forces us in a certain pattern. So language uses us—right? I do not know if you have noticed it. When you use the words *Communism* or *Socialism* or *Capitalism* or *Catholic, Protestant, Hindu, Jew,* and so on, they act upon us and force us to think in certain ways—right? So language is driving us, using us. I don't know if you are aware of it. And if you use language—not allow it to drive you—then you are using words without any emotional content. Then there is a possibility of exact communication. Are we getting somewhere together? Please understand this because we are going to go into something that—I think, I am not sure yet—will come out of all our inquiry into freedom, from our awareness that identity destroys freedom, curtails freedom, limits freedom. And if you are satisfied with that limitation of freedom then you must also be aware of its consequences, which are separation, continual lack of relationship, effort, war, violence, and all the rest of it.

And in inquiring into ourselves we must also be very clearly aware that language is not driving us; that when we use the word *Communism* we kind of withdraw from it emotionally. Or if you are so inclined the capitalist world of America and so on, again the same thing. So one must be aware very seriously, if you at all want to go into all this, which I am not urging you to do, that language is not driving us, then we can use words in their simplicity, in their meaning without any emotional content. Then you and I are in constant communication—right? Can you do this? Not tomorrow, now? Then we can proceed together, not at a slow pace, but galloping along.

There is only freedom when there is absolute non-identification with anything, with the church, with the gods, with beliefs, with a statue—you follow?—with anything! You say something to me, you use cruel words and you call me a name. I am hurt. And most human beings in the world are hurt, not only physiologically but much more psychologically. You are hurt, aren't you? And from that hurt we do all kinds of things: resist, withdraw, fear, become violent or bitter, and so on and so on and so on. This hurt, if you examine it very closely, is the movement of thought in the formation of the image—right? Thought has created an image about oneself, that one is beautiful, that one is intellectually marvellous, that one is, and so on and so on. And when you use an ugly word, angrily point out something, that image gets hurt; which is thought—please follow all this—thought that has created an image about itself; that image gets hurt. Can one live right throughout life without a single hurt? Then only is there freedom, then only is there sanity.

Brockwood Park,
12 September 1978

I THINK MOST of us are slaves, either to religious concepts, beliefs, and symbols, or to some kind of experience, or slaves to institutions, and concepts. And being prisoners to all that, how can one be a light to oneself? If one is committed to a certain pattern of life, a certain way of living, if one is a businessman or a scientist or a philosopher, one is caught in that; one becomes completely absorbed in it and the rest of life flows by. We are concerned in our discussion with the whole of life, not just one part, one segment, or one particular tendency, or one's profession. So does one realize, including myself, that one is caught in a routine, which naturally prevents freedom? It prevents freedom and so one can never be clear in oneself. One can never understand the depth of oneself when one is dependent on something; one cannot be a light to oneself.

Intelligence, Computers, and the Mechanical Mind

From The Way of Intelligence, *Rishi Valley,*
4 December 1980

CAN WE MOVE to something else, which is, pleasure is always in the known? I have no pleasure today but the day after tomorrow it might happen. I like to think it will happen. I don't know if you see what I mean. Pleasure is a time movement. Is there pleasure that is not based on knowledge? My whole life is the known. I project the known into the future modifying it, but it is still the known. I have no pleasure in the unknown. And the computer is in the field of the known. Now the real question is whether there is freedom from the known. That is the real question because pleasure is there, suffering is there, fear is there, the whole movement of the mind is the known. And it may project the unknown, theorize, but that is not a fact. So computers, chemicals, genetics, cloning are all the known. So can there be freedom from the known? The known is destroying man. The astrophysicists are going to space from the known. They are pursuing the investigation of the heavens, the cosmos, through instruments constructed by thought, and they are looking through those instruments and discovering the universe, watching what it is; it is still the known.

Questioner: A very interesting thing struck me just now. The present mind of man, in the way it is functioning, is threatened. It is being destroyed. Either the machine takes it over and it is destroyed, or the other freedom from the known will also destroy its present functioning. The challenge is much deeper.

Krishnamurti: Yes. That is what I said. You got it. What you are saying is, if I understand rightly, the known in which our minds are functioning is destroying us. The known is also the future projections as the machine, drugs, genetics, cloning, all that is born out of these. So both are destroying us.

Q: She is also saying the mind of man has always moved in the known, in pursuit of pleasure. That has resulted in technology that will destroy it. Then she is saying that the other movement, which is freedom from the known, will also destroy the mind as we know it now.

K: Yes. Freedom from the known? What are you saying?

Q: There are two movements, she says. The movement of the known is leading to greater and greater destruction of the mind. The way out is freedom from the known, which is also destroying the movement of the known.

K: Wait. Freedom is not from something. It is an ending. Do you follow?

Q: Are you saying, sir, that this freedom from the known is of such a nature that you are not destroying this movement, that thought has its place, mind has its place? Are you saying in that there is freedom?

K: I say there is only freedom, but not from the known.

Q: I say the mind is functioning in a particular way, what we call the human mind operates in a certain way. That human mind is put under pressure by technological advances. This other, freedom from the known, also is totally destructive of this function of the mind. Therefore, a new mind—whether born of technology or one that is free of the known—is inevitable. They are the only two things; the present position is out.

K: Let us be clear. Either there must be a new mind or the present thing is going to destroy the mind. Right? But the new mind can only exist actually, not theoretically; it can only exist when knowledge ends. Knowledge has created the machine, and we live on knowledge. We are machines; we are now separating the two. The machine is destroying us. The machine is the product of knowledge; we are the product of knowledge. Therefore, knowledge is destroying us, not the machine. So, the question then is: Can knowledge end? Not, Can there be freedom from knowledge? Then you are avoiding or escaping from knowledge.

Q: The question is: Can knowledge or the action born of knowledge end? Action out of knowledge can end. Knowledge can't end.

K: It can.

Q: Action out of knowledge?

K: Action is freedom from knowledge.

Q: Knowledge can't end.

K: Yes, sir.

Q: What do you mean when you say all knowledge ends?

Q: There is only knowledge?

K: There is only knowledge, not the ending of knowledge. I don't know if I am making myself clear.

Q: So, sir, there is the tremendous force of self-preservation and there is only knowledge. And you are asking, can knowledge end, which means self-annihilation?

K: No, I understand what you are saying. I am leaving now, for the moment, the ending of the self. I am saying the computer, which includes all technology, and my life are based on knowledge. So there is no division between the two.

Q: I follow that.

K: This is a tremendous thing. And so long as we are living in knowledge, our brain is being destroyed through routine, the machine, and so on. So the mind is knowledge. There is no question of saying it must free itself from knowledge. See that. There is only the mind which is knowledge. I am going to tell you something. You see, you have blocked yourself. Don't say it is impossible. If you say it is impossible, you couldn't have invented the computers. Move from there. The mind when it says it must be free, whatever it does, is within the field of knowledge. So what is the state of the mind that is completely aware, or knows, or is cognizant that it is entirely knowledge?

I have moved. Don't you see it? Now what has taken place?

Apparently knowledge is movement. Knowledge has been acquired through movement. So knowledge is movement. So time, all that, is movement.

Q: You are speaking of the state of mind when time comes to a stop.

K: That is freedom. Time is movement. Which means what? It is very interesting, sir. Let me put it together. Mind has invented the computer. I have used the word to include all that technology, genetics, cloning, chemicals. That is born from the knowledge that man has acquired. It is still the known, the product of the known, with its hypotheses, theory, and refuting the theory and all that. Man has also done exactly the same thing as the machine. So there is no division between the two. The mind is knowledge. Whatever it does will be born of knowledge—man's gods, his temples are born of knowledge. Knowledge is a movement. Can the movement stop?

That is really freedom. That means perception is free from knowledge and action is not out of knowledge. Perception of the snake, the danger is action, but that perception is based on centuries of conditioning about the snake. The perception that I am a Hindu, which has gone on for three thousand years, is the same movement. And we are living in that field all the time. That is destructive, not the machine. Unless that machine of the mind stops—not the computer—we are going to destroy ourselves.

So is there a perception that is not born out of knowledge? Because when this movement stops, there must be action.

The Future of Man

From The Way of Intelligence, *Chapter 3*
New Delhi, 5 November 1981

IN THE WORLD, there is great disturbance, corruption; people are very, very disturbed. It is dangerous to walk on the streets. When we are talking about freedom from fear, we want outward freedom, freedom from chaos, anarchy, or dictatorship. But we never demand or inquire if there is an inner freedom at all: freedom of the mind. Is that freedom actual or theoretical? We regard the State as an impediment to freedom. Communists and other totalitarian people say there is no such thing as freedom; the State, the government, is the only authority. And they are suppressing every form of freedom. So what kind of freedom do we want? Out there? Outside of us? Or inward freedom? When we talk about freedom, is it the freedom of choice between this government and that, here and there, between outer and inner freedom? The inner psyche always conquers the outer. The psyche, that is, the inward structure of man—his thoughts, emotions, his ambitions, his actions, his greed—always conquers the outer. So where do we seek freedom? Can there be freedom from nationality that gives us a sense of security? Can there be freedom from all the superstitions, dogmas, and religions? A new civilization can only come about through real religion, not through superstition, dogma, or traditional religions.

Saanen, 10 July 1984

WE SHOULD INQUIRE into what are freedom, health, and the quality of energy that comes when one captures or sees, perceives the truth of all time contained in the now. Right? What is freedom? All human beings throughout the ages have sought some kind of freedom, historically, religiously, and so on. And freedom is translated now as doing exactly what one wants, which obviously you are all doing, as having choice—one can choose to go from one place to another place, from one job to another job, unless you are where there is total dictatorship and everything is controlled. There even your thinking, feeling is moulded according to pattern. So there is a denial in the totalitarian states of freedom, therefore such states are retrogressive—you understand? Going back, not moving.

We must inquire into what is freedom? Is freedom choice? To choose between two cars, between two materials, to go where you want, to fulfill yourself at the expense of everybody else—right? To try to become much more than we are—better, nobler, wiser, acquiring more knowledge—which is the whole process of becoming, which is called fulfilling. "I must fulfil." "I must have roots somewhere." You follow? The implication of all that is becoming. Not only physical becoming, from an employee to an owner, from an apprentice to a master, but also to feel I am becoming inwardly. "I am this, I will be that. I am envious, greedy, violent"—

we will use the word violent, we are violent. "I will one day achieve non-violence." Perhaps in a year or two, or perhaps at the end of my life when I am just about to die—right? And all this implies a psychological becoming. That's clear. And is there freedom in becoming? You understand my question? Or is freedom something entirely different? Please, together we are investigating, exploring. I am not explaining and you are just receiving. Together we are inquiring, which demands that you exercise your brain, not accept a thing, not accept whatever the speaker says. Therefore the inquiry must be yours, not the speaker's. The speaker may just outline, put it into words but the activity, the penetration, must be on your part. So we are both sharing in this—right? Not I put something forward with which you agree or disagree—that implies no sharing. But are we both inquiring, probing, asking, doubting everything we think and feel, and its relationship to time, and seeing if that becoming prevents freedom—right? Are we together in this a little bit? May I explain it more?

That is, if one is a teacher who wants gradually to become a professor in a university, or an apprentice in any discipline, he is all the time attempting to become something—becoming more, becoming a greater expert, with greater skill, greater knowledge. This energy given to a certain subject is limited. Therefore that denies freedom. You understand? Are we together in this somewhat?

You see we don't really demand freedom. We demand it only within the limited area in which I must do what I feel, I must act according to my like and dislike, and in that action I am free; I can choose between you and another, and so on. So all that activity is very, very limited, and that very limitation denies freedom. Of course! We are also verbally limited, linguistically we are limited. Let's find out whether language limits freedom. The speaker is using English—that language, the words, condition the brain and therefore it becomes limited. Does language condition the brain, or does language not limit the brain, condition the brain? You are inquiring? Please go into it with me. If there were only you and the speaker together and not such a large audience, just you, my friend and myself, then we could discuss it very, very closely. And I am going to do that—right? That is, you represent my friend and I represent the speaker. The speaker and the friend are discussing this question: does freedom lie in becoming something all the time? Does freedom lie in expressing your ambition? Does freedom lie in trying to fulfil your own desires? And the friend says, "I really don't understand what the devil you are talking about. We are used to this; our conditioning, our habit, is this. We are always wanting to fulfil, to become, both in the outer world and also in the inner world. We must achieve something otherwise there is no progress" and so on. My friend is saying this, countering everything I am saying, that the speaker is saying. And the speaker says, don't get so excited about it, let's look at it together. When you are ambitious, both in the external world and in the psychological world, ambition is the same whether you are ambitious to become tremendously rich or ambitious to reach Nirvana, Heaven, or illumination, or ambitious to become silent. And that ambition, the speaker is saying to his friend, is limited, is not freedom. And we have misused that word *freedom*. Each person is trying to assert himself, aggressively holding on to his opinion, judgment, evaluation, dogma, creed, and so on. And all this we call freedom. And is that freedom? My friend says, "I begin to understand what you are talking about. I agree." I say, don't agree but see the fact of it, the truth of it—right?

So freedom must be something entirely different. And is it possible to come to that, to realize that freedom? That is not to be ambitious at all. Go into it, which doesn't prevent the love of doing—right? The scientists throughout the world are very ambitious too, like the rest of us. They want to achieve some superior armaments against the Russians and so on. All that game, that horrible game they are playing. So every human being in the world, however uneducated, stupid, terribly intellectual, is always caught in this process. And that is generally called freedom. And the speaker says that is not freedom. And the friend says, "Does language prevent, or encourage the limited activity of the brain?" You are following all this? Does this interest you? Are you quite sure? Or is it that you are playing a game with me? Does language condition the brain? It does condition the brain if the words become important. Whether the words are English words, or French words, or German, or Italian, or Russian, when the word has lost its depth, when the word is used casually, when the word has special significance for each one, when the words have become the network of the brain— you understand? Are you following?—then the words condition the brain. Right? But when the words are used for communication purposes, which requires a certain sensitivity, attention, pliability, affection, then words can be used without their limiting quality. Then the brain is not conditioned by words. But as we are now, words do condition our brain. When you say, "the totalitarian states," I immediately have a picture of it. You immediately see various dictators in different parts of the world, because their pictures have been in every newspaper for the last fifty years. The image springs up and that image conditions the brain. You are following all this? When I use the word guru (laughter)—there you are, you have a reaction immediately! Or when a word like the Christ is used to a Christian—immediately. Or to a Hindu with his particular word, or the Buddhist. Please see the importance of the linguistic conditioning, and whether in that conditioning all kinds of troubles arise, all kinds of conflicts arise—the Hindu conflict with the Moslem, the Moslem and the Arab with the Jew, the Christians who believe in god with the totalitarians—you follow? This is going on.

So is it possible to be free from the linguistic prison? You understand? Sirs, you don't put your minds to all this. Right? See if it is possible for you, sitting here now, to be entirely free of the image of words. So there is no freedom in becoming. There is no freedom when a man or a woman is ambitious, greedy, envious. He may think he is free because he expresses his ambition, but there is no freedom in becoming. And there is no freedom when the brain is caught or imprisoned in words with their images.

❖

SO INQUIRE INTO freedom, inquire into what health is, because if you are not healthy you cannot have freedom, because that will impede you. I may be paralyzed but I can still be healthy—you understand? I may have only one eye to see clearly, but that doesn't stop me being healthy. Health is destroyed by this constant conflict, achievement, success, ambition, uncertainty, confusion, all the pain of life. And energy, energy is dissipated. You understand, sirs? By chattering, arguing, holding on to what you have done and saying: "This is right, I am going to stick to it." You understand? Energy implies constant movement, constantly discovering something new, not technologically, but psychologically. So that your brain becomes extraordinarily active and does not dissipate that energy. When you have that energy then you can look at problems—you understand? And understand time. All problems dovetail, they all fit together, they are not separate. It is one long steady movement.

Brockwood Park, 31 August 1985

As WE SAID previously, we are rather serious, at least the speaker is. He has been at it for the last seventy years or more. And just attending a couple of talks, or reading some printed words is not going to solve our problems, it is not going to help us. And the speaker is not trying to help you. Please be convinced of that, be assured that the speaker is no authority, and therefore he is not a person to whom you can turn to be helped. There are others who might help you. And if you want to be helped, if one may point out most respectfully, then you leave your problems to be solved by others, and they will solve them according to their desires, self-interest, their power, their position, and all that business. So we are ordinary laymen talking together. We are going to inquire together, face the facts, not the ideas about the fact but facts. And not ide-ologies, they are meaningless. Not theories, speculations, who is illumined, who is not, who is—what?—nearer to god than you, but together we are going to go into this question of freedom, what relationship freedom has to time and time to thought and action. Because we live by action, everything we do is action, not a partic-ular action in the business world, or in the scientific world, or in the speculative world called philosophy. But rather we are going to look at things as they are.

There is a great deal of anarchy in the world, chaos, disorder, and who has brought this about? That is our first question. Who is responsible for all the mess that we have in the world, economically, socially, politically, and so on, all leading up to war? There are wars going on, terrible wars now. And do we each one of us realize not intellectually but actually in our daily life, the state of the house in which we live, not only the house built by man outside, but the house inside. Do we realize how disorderly it is, contradictory, how very little freedom we have? That word *freedom* also implies love, not just freedom to do what you like, when you like, where you like. But we are living on this earth, all of us, and each one is seeking his own freedom, his own expression, his own fulfillment, his own path to enlightenment, whatever that be: his own particular form of religion, superstition, belief, faith and all the things that go with it, authority, hierarchical authority, politically, religiously, and so on. So we have very little freedom. And that word, which is so freely used by every psychopath and every human being, whether he lives in Russia, where the tyranny is appalling, or in the so-called democratic world, every human being inwardly, consciously or unconsciously, needs freedom, like every tree in the world needs freedom to grow, to have that sense of the quality of dignity, love.

And what is the relationship of freedom to self-interest? Please, we are talking things over together, you are not, if I may point out, listening to a speaker, listening to a man on the platform. He is not important at all. And the speaker really means this; he, the speaker, is not important. But perhaps you might give your ear to what he says as though two friends are talking over things very seriously. We are asking: What is the relationship between freedom and self-interest? Where do you draw the line between freedom and self-interest? And what is self-interest? What is its relationship to thought and to time? Please, all these questions are involved in freedom. Bearing in mind that freedom is not fulfilling one's own ambitions, greed, envy, and so on. What is the relationship of self-interest to freedom? You know what self-interest is? Self-interest may hide under every stone of our life—right? Are we talking together? Are you quite sure we are talking together—not with somebody higher up but all of us sitting on the same level?

What is self-interest? Can one consciously, deliberately, inquire into that? How deep it is, how superficial, where it is necessary, where it totally, completely, has no place at all. You understand my question, we are together questioning. Self-interest has brought about a great deal of confusion in the world, a great deal of disorder, confusion, conflict. Whether that self-interest be identified with a country, with a community, with a family, or with god, with the beliefs, the faiths and so on, it is all self-interest, seeking enlightenment—for god's sake, as though you can seek it! Also in that search there is self-interest, and also there is self-interest when you build a house, have insurance, mortgages. The self-interest is encouraged commercially, and also by all religions; they talk about liberation but self-interest comes first. And we have to live in this world, we have to function, have to earn money, have children, be married or not married. And living in this world of the twentieth century how deep, or how superficial is our self-interest? It is important to inquire into this. Self-interest divides people—right? We and they, you and I, my interest as opposed to your interest, my family interests oppose your family interests, your country, my country in which I have invested a great deal of emotion and physical interest for which I am willing to fight and kill, which is war. And we invest our interest in ideas, faith, beliefs, dogmas, in rituals and so on, this whole cycle. At the root of it there is a great deal of self-interest.

Now can one live in this world daily, clearly, with self-interest where it is necessary—please I am using this word carefully—where it is physically necessary and psychologically, inwardly, it is totally abandoned? Is that possible? You understand? Are we together? Is it possible for each one of us living here in a very, very complex society, competitive, divided by agreement and disagreement, one faith opposing another faith, this great division that is going on, not only individually but collectively, and living in this world to draw the line between self-interest and no self-interest whatsoever psychologically? Can we do that? You can talk about it endlessly, as we like to go to talks and lectures and listen to somebody, but here we have to observe together, you have not only to listen to each other verbally but also deeply, inwardly find out extensively, not just my self-interest, extensively, wholly, where self-interest lies. And inwardly, psychologically, can one live without any kind of muttering of self-interest, of the self, the "me," which is the essence of self-interest? Another can't explain, or say this is self-interest, this is not self-interest, that would be terrible. But one can find out for oneself, very carefully inquiring step by step, hesitantly, not coming to any conclusion. Because there is nobody who is going to help us. I think we must be completely assured that nobody is going to help us. They may pretend and you may pretend, but the actuality is that after these two and half million years, or forty thousand years, we are still seeking help, and we are stuck. We are coming to the end of our tether.

And in the inquiry into self-interest we have also to go into the question: what is freedom? And freedom implies love; freedom does not mean irresponsibility, doing exactly what one wants, which has brought about such a mess in the world. And also what relationship has self-interest to thought? We went into the question of time the other day, and also thought, thinking. Shall we go into it briefly, what time and thought are—need we? It is no good repeating it over and over again, it gets rather monotonous, for the speaker at least. So he has to vary the words, the special phrasing, the silence between the phrases. But if you merely listen to words, words, words and don't act—then we will be left only with ashes.

Sources and Acknowledgments

From the Verbatim Report of the eighth public talk in Bombay, 7 March 1948, in *Collected Works of J. Krishnamurti*, copyright © 1991 Krishnamurti Foundation of America, pages 1-5.

From the Verbatim Report of the third public talk in Bangalore, 18 July 1948, in *Collected Works of J. Krishnamurti*, copyright © 1991 Krishnamurti Foundation of America, pages 6-7.

From the Verbatim Report of the third public talk in Poona, 31 January 1953, in *Collected Works of J. Krishnamurti*, copyright © 1991 Krishnamurti Foundation of America, pages 8-11.

From the Verbatim Report of the ninth public talk in Bombay, 8 March 1953, in *Collected Works of J. Krishnamurti*, copyright © 1991 Krishnamurti Foundation of America, pages 12-14.

From the Verbatim Report of the thirteenth talk with students at Rajghat School, Varanasi, 20 January 1954, in *Collected Works of J. Krishnamurti*, copyright © 1991 Krishnamurti Foundation of America, pages 15-16.

From the Verbatim Report of the fifth public talk in Poona, 21 September 1958, in *Collected Works of J. Krishnamurti*, copyright © 1990 Krishnamurti Foundation of America, pages 17-19.

From the Verbatim Report of the third public talk in Bombay, 3 December 1958, in *Collected Works of J. Krishnamurti*, copyright © 1991 Krishnamurti Foundation of America, pages 20-24.

From the Verbatim Report of the sixth public talk in Bombay,

14 December 1958, in *Collected Works of J. Krishnamurti*, copyright © 1991 Krishnamurti Foundation of America, pages 25-31.

From the Verbatim Report of the first public talk in Madras, 22 November 1959, in *Collected Works of J. Krishnamurti*, copyright © 1991 Krishnamurti Foundation of America, pages 32-39.

From the Verbatim Report of the first public talk in Bombay, 23 December 1959, in *Collected Works of J. Krishnamurti*, copyright © 1991 Krishnamurti Foundation of America, pages 40-41.

From the Verbatim Report of the first public talk in Varanasi, 24 January 1960, in *Collected Works of J. Krishnamurti*, copyright © 1991 Krishnamurti Foundation of America, pages 42-44.

From the Verbatim Report of the first public talk at Ojai, 21 May 1960, in *Collected Works of J. Krishnamurti*, copyright © 1991 Krishnamurti Foundation of America, pages 45-51.

From the Verbatim Report of the first public talk in Varanasi, 1 January 1962, in *Collected Works of J. Krishnamurti*, copyright © 1991 Krishnamurti Foundation of America, pages 52-59.

From the Verbatim Report of the eighth public talk in New Delhi, 14 February 1962, in *Collected Works of J. Krishnamurti*, copyright © 1991 Krishnamurti Foundation of America, page 60.

From the Verbatim Report of the fifth public talk at Saanen, 31 July 1962, in *Collected Works of J. Krishnamurti*, copyright © 1991 Krishnamurti Foundation of America, pages 61-64.

From the Verbatim Report of the third public talk at Saanen, 11 July 1963, in *Collected Works of J Krishnamurti*, copyright © 1991 Krishnamurti Foundation of America, pages 65-68.

From the Verbatim Report of the second public talk in Madras, 15 January 1964, in *Collected Works of J. Krishnamurti*, copyright © 1991 Krishnamurti Foundation of America, pages 69-71.

From the Verbatim Report of the third public talk in Bombay, 16 February 1964, in *Collected Works of J. Krishnamurti*, copyright © 1991 Krishnamurti Foundation of America, pages 72-77.

From the Verbatim Report of the seventh public talk in Bombay,